BECOMING A GLOBALLY COMPETENT SCHOOL LEADER

Ariel **Tichnor-Wagner**

BECOMING A GLOBALLY COMPETENT SCHOOL LEADER

ASCD

Alexandria, Virginia USA

1703 N. Beauregard St. • Alexandria, VA 22311-1714 USA
Phone: 800-933-2723 or 703-578-9600 • Fax: 703-575-5400
Website: www.ascd.org • E-mail: member@ascd.org
Author guidelines: www.ascd.org/write

Ranjit Sidhu, *Executive Director and CEO*; Stefani Roth, *Publisher*; Genny Ostertag, *Director, Content Acquisitions*; Allison Scott, *Acquisitions Editor*; Julie Houtz, *Director, Book Editing & Production*; Jamie Greene, *Associate Editor*; Judi Connelly, *Senior Art Director*; Donald Ely, *Associate Art Director*; Kelly Marshall, *Interim Manager, Production Services*; Tristan Coffelt, *Senior Production Specialist*; Keith Demmons, *Senior Production Designer*; Shajuan Martin, *E-Publishing Specialist*

PAPERBACK ISBN: 978-1-4166-2850-7   ASCD product #119011

PDF E-BOOK ISBN: 978-1-4166-2852-1; see Books in Print for other formats.

Quantity discounts: 10–49, 10%; 50+, 15%; 1,000+, special discounts (e-mail programteam@ascd.org or call 800-933-2723, ext. 5773, or 703-575-5773). For desk copies, go to www.ascd.org/deskcopy.

Library of Congress Cataloging-in-Publication Data
Names: Tichnor-Wagner, Ariel, author.
Title: Becoming a globally competent school leader / by Ariel Tichnor-Wagner.
Description: Alexandria, VA : ASCD, [2020] | "ASCD product #11901" | Includes bibliographical references and index.
Identifiers: LCCN 2019048643 (print) | LCCN 2019048644 (ebook) | ISBN 9781416628507 (paperback) | ISBN 9781416628521 (pdf)
Subjects: LCSH: School administrators—Training of. | Educational leadership. | Education and globalization. | International education.
Classification: LCC LB1738.5 .T54 2020 (print) | LCC LB1738.5 (ebook) | DDC 371.2—dc23
LC record available at https://lccn.loc.gov/2019048643
LC ebook record available at https://lccn.loc.gov/2019048644

27 26 25 24 23 22 21 20   1 2 3 4 5 6 7 8 9 10 11 12

BECOMING A GLOBALLY COMPETENT SCHOOL LEADER

Acknowledgments

Deep and sustained school change doesn't happen overnight. It takes commitment, a whole lot of time, and teamwork. The same holds true for writing books.

The seed of the idea that germinated into this book began swirling around when I was completing my doctoral studies in the School of Education at the University of North Carolina at Chapel Hill. During this time, I was working with a team of researchers to develop and validate the Globally Competent Learning Continuum, an online self-reflection tool and resource repository to help educators of all grade levels and subject areas develop globally competent teaching practices. As I observed and interviewed globally committed teachers in very different classroom contexts, a common sentiment emerged: teachers yearned for more support from school administrators. Yes, principals appreciated the rigorous and relevant learning being brought into the classroom, but they did not yet have expertise in how to support globally competent teaching so that it could spread in a systemic way throughout the school. Unfortunately, professional learning opportunities that explicitly targeted globally competent school leadership were few and far between.

This book seeks to help fill that gap and sustain a conversation about leading the charge in transforming schools into globally relevant and culturally sustaining spaces. In many ways, this is a companion to *Becoming a Globally Competent Teacher*, coauthored by me, Hillary Parkhouse, Jocelyn Glazier, and J.

Montana Cain, as it provides school leaders—from principals to instructional coaches to teachers—the knowledge and skillset to cultivate a culture and climate conducive to developing, implementing, spreading, and sustaining programs and practices that prepare students to thrive in our diverse, interconnected world.

Thank you to ASCD for bringing this conversation to the forefront of education, believing in its importance, and providing me with a home to create this work. A special thank you to Allison Scott and Jamie Greene for their editorial eye—and patience!

The research upon which this book is based comes from two main sources. First is my dissertation research on the evolution, implementation, and adoption of global education policy. I humbly thank the 30+ school and district leaders who opened their calendars, offices, and schools to me. Their experiences informed the leadership-as-implementation framework that organizes much of this book, along with numerous examples of what globally competent leadership looks like on the ground in different community settings. A special thank you to my friends at World View and Participate (formerly VIF International Education) who helped forge many of these initial introductions and provided great insight into how global education programming is implemented across diverse contexts.

A second basis for this work comes from my research for the ASCD and Longview Foundation project Globally Competent Educational Leadership: A Framework for Leading Schools in a Diverse, Interconnected World. I hold a huge amount of appreciation for Jennifer Manise, a great thought partner and collaborator, in devising and gathering the right people in the room to operationalize a set of tenets for school leaders committed to global competence. I am especially grateful to the many, many teachers, principals, education leaders, and global education thought leaders who provided crucial insights into what these attributes are—and who are living and breathing this work every day. Your work is contributing to making the world a more peaceful, sustainable home for all of us who inhabit it, and it is an honor to share your collective wisdom.

Finally, this book would not be without the two most incredible people whom I have ever met: Adina and Eliana. I have been working on this book for literally their entire lives (but, in all fairness, they are only 3 and 1 as I write this). There have been times when I did not know if I would have the hours in the day or the energy to get this manuscript to press. But each time I read a headline about the latest trade war, UN climate report, or human rights violation at the border; felt the fear and sorrow following a shooting at a house of worship, school, or workplace; or witnessed the hope and energy of people coming together in global marches or acts of local volunteerism, I knew that I owed you, and your generation, this much. My hope is that when you enter kindergarten, your public education will inspire and empower you to make a positive glocal impact.

Leading with the World in Mind

One child, one teacher, one book, one pen can change the world.

Malala Yousafzai

Consider what the world looks like for our children in schools today. They are hyperconnected digital natives who have only known a world where, with a touch or swipe of a pocket-sized screen, we can instantly communicate with anyone, anywhere; find whatever information we need; and buy any product we want. Although this technology has all but eliminated geographic divides, it has also introduced invisible digital barriers, filtering what we see through conscious and subconscious social, cultural, and political leanings. We don't think twice as we walk down supermarket aisles and see shrimp from China, peppers and avocadoes from Mexico, and bananas from Costa Rica. We take the inexpensive cost of our clothes for granted—a price that is kept low through a carefully orchestrated global supply chain of raw materials, labor, and distribution. We have lived through natural disasters and unpredictable weather patterns barraging huge swathes of our planet. It is no wonder that political and military leaders describe the only world that our youth have ever known as volatile, uncertain, complex, and ambiguous.

What will our world look like when our youngest students graduate? Will they be navigating a dystopic reality where robots rule supreme, water has overrun once-populated urban centers, and nuclear warheads fly through the sky? Or will they feel secure, knowing that they'll be able to provide for themselves and their families, that violent conflicts between nations and ethnic groups are declining, and technology is being harnessed to protect the planet's environment and natural resources? The jobs, climate, and international alliances in our not-so-distant-future are anyone's guess.

What does all of this have to do with schools?

Everything.

Society writ large has long seen schools as vital institutions for preparing students for citizenship and careers. Education historian David Labaree (1997) wrote that schools occupy "the intersection between what we hope society will become and what we think it really is" (p. 41). In the early years of the United States, public schools were forged as spaces for political socialization for democratic participation in a republican government and for creating a national culture and sense of patriotism in a country with diverse religious, ethnic, racial, religious, and political groups. Over the years, schools have also been seen as a silver bullet for improving society's many ailments and as economic engines that bolster the human capital of nations and increase competitiveness for jobs and wealth in a global economy (Labaree, 1997; Spring, 2010; Tichnor-Wagner & Socol, 2016). The exact goals of school may be contested—a way to socialize youth for democratic citizenship, bolster economic growth by creating a knowledgeable and well-trained workforce, or provide individuals with a chance to compete for jobs in a competitive marketplace. But there is agreement that education should equip students with the requisite knowledge and skills for the world outside the schoolhouse doors as engaged citizens and productive workers.

Nevertheless, in many ways, how students experience school has not caught up with the world in which we currently live. One-fifth of the way through the 21st century, our system of schooling is still locked in early 20th-century thinking. Issues that people everywhere face—climate change, spread of diseases, food insecurity—require interdisciplinary solutions. Yet schools are predominately organized by single-subject courses and high-stakes tests that emphasize core subject areas of reading, math, and science. According to the U.S. Census Bureau, 65.5 million residents speak a language other than English at home. Yet schools in the United States are predominately monolingual. Researchers estimate that only 3 percent of elementary school students are enrolled in some form of bilingual education (Goldenberg & Wagner, 2015). Even foreign language courses are in short supply. Only 20 percent of U.S. students are enrolled in foreign language programs, and only 15 percent of public schools offer them (American Academy of Arts & Sciences, 2017).

As education historians David Tyack and Larry Cuban (1995) argue, "Change where it counts the most—in the daily interactions of teachers and students—is the hardest to achieve and the most important" (p.10). With that in mind, what should teaching and learning look like to remain relevant and engaging and to truly prepare students for the world? And how can educators lead the necessary changes to make that vision a reality?

A 21st Century Education Grounded in Our World

A Crisis of Relevancy

Schools today face a crisis of relevancy. There is a disconnect between the skills and knowledge students feel they need to navigate and shape the current realities in which they live and what schools are currently offering. The result is, inevitably, student disengagement. A 2015 Gallup Poll found that only half of adolescents felt engaged in school, and one in five reported that they were actively disengaged (Gallup Inc., 2015). This disengagement, in turn, can lead to lower academic performance and higher dropout rates.

On Friday, March 15, 2019, millions of students skipped school in order to protest for action around climate change. That same day, Terry Godwaldt, the director of the Centre for Global Education in Edmonton, Canada, spoke to a group of educators at a global leadership summit at ASCD's annual Empower conference and asked a simple yet profound question: "Why do students have to step out the classroom to make change?"

The answer is simple. Schools are not doing enough to address the realities that students face in their current and future lives. The following section delineates some of the economic, social, and environmental realities that swirl around schools yet deeply affect the everyday lives of youth.

Economic Realities

When students graduate, they will compete for jobs in a global, knowledge-based economy. As Linda Darling-Hammond (2010) illustrates, "Globalization is changing everything about how we work, how we communicate, and ultimately, how we live. Employers can distribute their activities around the entire globe, based on the costs and skills of workers in nearly any nation that has built an infrastructure for transportation and communications. Customers in the United States buy their clothes from China and the Philippines and have their questions about the new computer they bought answered by workers in India" (p. 4).

One in five jobs in the United States is tied to international trade. From 1992 until 2016, trade-dependent jobs increased by 148 percent, covering a wide range of industries from agriculture to manufacturing to financial services to higher education (Baughman & Francois, 2018). Products we consume as part of our everyday lives—the fruit in our refrigerators, the phones in our pockets, the cars we drive to work—depend on global supply chains. As automation and artificial intelligence take over manual jobs once performed by people, the need for schools to focus on what makes us uniquely *human—*emotional intelligence, storytelling, the arts—becomes more acute.

Cultural Pluralism

Migration is as old as humankind. Today, of course, it is happening at a far faster rate than with our ancestors, who took tens of thousands of years to traverse continents by foot. Globally, over 244 million people live in a country different from where they were born. The push-and-pull factors that drive people to move across boundaries are complex, though many migrants are driven by prospects of work. Global displacement has also hit record numbers, with the number of refugees displaced by war, persecution, a profound lack of economic security and opportunity, environmental degradation, and natural disasters topping over 22 million (International Organization for Migration, 2017). As people migrate, they carry with them their languages, religions, values, foods, and other cultural signifiers, therefore adding new richness to the diversity of already pluralistic societies.

In the United States, about one in four children under the age of 18 are first- or second-generation immigrants (Child Trends, 2018), and nearly one in four public school students speak a language other than English at home (Zeigler & Camarota, 2018). Shifting migration patterns over the past few decades have resulted in an increase in immigrant populations—and from a greater diversity of places—in previously homogenous states, cities, and towns. For example, historically speaking, a majority of immigrants ultimately settled in only a handful of states (California, New York, Florida, Texas, New Jersey, Illinois, and Massachusetts). However, since 2000, immigrants have increasingly moved to the central and southeast regions of the country, where immigration rates rose by double the national average (Terrazas, 2011). In these communities, schools have suddenly become microcosms of newly diversified communities.

What "diversity" looks like over time has also changed. The first European colonizers who arrived to what is now the United States in the 17th and 18th centuries mainly spoke English, German, French, Dutch, and Spanish, and they brought with them enslaved Africans with rich and varied cultures and languages that survived through the shackles of slavery. The land these colonizers settled was by no means an empty wilderness but a landscape of over 15 million people representing more than 500 indigenous groups and many more dialects (Dunbar-Ortiz, 2014; Garcia, 2009). The mid to late 19th century saw a stripping away of indigenous people from their lands and culture, as the U.S. government forced assimilation through education. Beginning in 1879, the U.S. government established boarding schools for Native American children that prescribed an English curriculum and forbade native languages.

Stringent immigration legislation in the late 19th and early 20th century limited the number of newcomers, heavily restricting those from southern and eastern Europe, China, and the rest of Asia and favoring northern European stock. It wasn't until the Immigration and Nationality Act of 1965 that these quotas were removed and more immigrants began arriving from Asia, Africa, and South and Central America. Today, a diverse immigrant community in the United States includes representation from around the world and every continent. Spanish speakers account for almost 80 percent of all nonnative English speakers in the country; over 400 other languages and dialects represent the rest (U.S. Department of Education, as cited in Garcia, 2009).

Renewed diversity has also caused a backlash against pluralism. Far-right nationalist populism has returned to the mainstream of politics in Europe, the United States, and Latin America, fueled by anti-immigrant and anti-foreign tropes and corresponding with a rise in hate crimes against religious, racial, and ethnic minorities. Youth are coming of age at a time of two competing visions of the future: one that rejects pluralism and one that embraces and empowers indigenous, immigrant, and other cultural groups as equal contributors to a diverse democracy.

Borderless Threats

The sustainability of our planet—and all of us—depends on cooperation among nations and the ability of people across geographic, cultural, and political divides to effectively collaborate and find solutions. Take, for example, the issue of climate change—or what many circles now call the climate crisis. Scientists predict that global temperatures will reach 1.5 degrees Celsius above preindustrial levels between 2030 and 2050 (Intergovernmental Panel on Climate Change, 2018). Though the impacts have been and will continue to be felt on all of Earth's ecosystems (e.g., extreme temperatures, heavy precipitation rates, extreme weather conditions, sea level change, species loss and extinction), future risks to health, livelihoods, food security, water supply, human security, and economic growth can be mitigated if the warming levels out at 1.5 degrees.

Reducing the effects of climate change will involve multilevel and cross-sectoral actions; contributions of public and private funds; new government policies; and education, information, community, and technological approaches (Intergovernmental Panel on Climate Change, 2018). The Paris Agreement, signed in 2016 and currently ratified by 125 nations, works on doing just that—by having nations agree to enact policy meant to limit greenhouse gas emissions and thereby curtail global temperature change (United Nations Climate Change, 2019).

The United Nations Sustainable Development Goals identify 17 global challenges that countries around the world face, with ambitious targets for attaining those goals. Goals include the elimination of poverty and hunger, good health and well-being among all people, access to high-quality education, gender equality, access to clean water and sanitation, proliferation of affordable and clean energy, availability of decent work and economic growth, industrial growth, an emphasis on innovation and infrastructure, reduced inequalities, growth of sustainable cities and communities, responsible consumption and production, climate action, protections for life below water and on land, and a strengthening of peace, justice, and institutions (United Nations, 2019).

Young people around the world are actively supporting these goals. The youth-led climate strikes in March and September of 2019, which has morphed into the weekly #FridaysforFuture movement to protest climate destruction, is but one example. Schools have an important role to play in helping students develop the skills, methods, and tools to advocate for a sustainable future.

Globally Competent Teaching and Learning: A Rigorous and Relevant Instructional Response

Against this backdrop, what outcomes should schools be striving for? Students need to develop a range of academic, social, and emotional competencies if they are to solve issues such as climate change, disease, and violent extremism that transcend national borders; live peacefully among neighbors in a culturally, politically, racially, ethnically, and religiously diverse society;

and thrive in a global knowledge-based economy. Youth already know this; it's time for schools to catch up.

Instead of one-dimensional measures of student success, schools need to focus on fostering the cognitive, behavioral, and social-emotional attributes students will actually need to survive and thrive in the real world. As stated in the culminating report of the Aspen Institute National Commission on Social, Emotional, and Academic Development (2019),

> There is a remarkable confluence of experience and science on one point: Children learn best when we treat them as human beings, with social and emotional as well as academic needs. . . . Children require a broad array of skills, attitudes, character traits, and values to succeed in school, careers, and life. . . . These social, emotional, and academic capacities are increasingly demanded in the American workplace, which puts a premium on the ability to work in diverse teams, grapple with difficult problems, and adjust to rapid change. (p. 5)

Global competence is a framework that fits this bill and helps educators balance social-emotional and academic learning goals. It is the set of dispositions, knowledge, and skills needed to live and work in a diverse, global society. Multiple definitions and frameworks around global competence exist (e.g., Mansilla & Jackson, 2011; OECD, 2018; Reimers, 2009a; UNESCO, 2015), but they all coalesce around the following social-emotional, cognitive, and behavioral domains:

1. Social-emotional: Dispositions of empathy, perspective recognition, and appreciation for diverse cultures.
2. Cognitive: Understanding global issues and trends, critical thinking, and problem solving.
3. Behavioral: Intercultural communication and collaboration, communicating in multiple languages and taking action on issues of local and global importance.

Figure 1.1 provides definitions of these vital learning outcomes for students in today's interconnected world.

A growing number of government agencies, nongovernmental organizations (NGOs), business leaders, and reform-minded educators have recognized the importance of and are advocating for making global competence an outcome for every student in all schools. A handful of state-level policies that support global competence development have been passed by state legislatures and departments of education. For example, the Illinois Global Scholars Certificate, passed by the state legislature and signed by the governor in 2017, awards a global scholar certification to high school students who complete global coursework, global service learning, and a performance-based capstone project in which they investigate and take action on a global issue.

North Carolina's state board of education approved a Global Educator Digital Badge in 2014, which awards teachers a digital badge for completing global professional development and a capstone project. This was followed in 2015 by the Global Ready School and Global Ready District designations that recognize schools and districts infusing global education across instruction, professional development, and partnerships. In addition, the Seal of Biliteracy, which recognizes students for attaining proficiency in English and another language by the time of graduation, is also becoming more popular in many states. As of 2017, 25 states and the District of Columbia participated in the program (Davin & Heineke, 2017).

The U.S. Department of Education has also recognized the importance of preparing a globally competent citizenry. Their 2012–2016 international strategy addressed the need to prepare all students to succeed globally through international education and engagement. Its first objective was to "increase global competencies for all U.S. students, including those from traditionally disadvantaged groups" (U.S. Department of Education, 2012, p. 5). The report argues,

Figure 1.1 | Global Competence Learning Outcomes

Outcomes	Definition
Social-Emotional	
Empathy	Identifying with others by seeing the world through their perspective.
Perspective recognition	Recognizing that one's perspective is not universally shared and that others hold perspectives that may be vastly different. Identifying the various influences that shape these perspectives.
Appreciation for diverse cultures	Acknowledging that the shared values, knowledge, and norms of a people or group vary and celebrating differences across an array of racial, ethnic, cultural, linguistic, religious, gender, and socioeconomic backgrounds.
Cognitive	
Global issues and trends	Understanding conditions and events pertinent to the lives of students, teachers, their local communities, country, and the wider world (e.g., environment, global health, human rights, economic and political development, world hunger, peace and conflict, racism, discrimination, and immigration).
Critical thinking	Examining possibilities carefully, fairly, and constructively by using higher-order thinking skills such as applying, analyzing, synthesizing, and evaluating information.
Problem solving	Finding solutions to difficult and complex issues.
Behavioral	
Intercultural communication	Respectfully interacting with people from different cultures so everyone understands one another. This includes verbal and nonverbal communication (e.g., speaking with someone in his or her native language, actively listening, being mindful of cultural interpretations of gestures and intonations).
Intercultural collaboration	Working in teams with people from diverse backgrounds toward a common goal so everyone feels valued, respected, and treated equally.
Taking action	Feeling a social responsibility to improve local and global conditions and taking concrete steps to do so.

In today's globalized world, an effective domestic education agenda must address global needs and trends and aim to develop a globally competent citizenry. It is no longer enough to focus solely on ensuring that our students have essential reading, writing, mathematics, and science skills. Our hyperconnected world also requires the ability to think critically and creatively to solve complex problems, the skills and dispositions to engage globally, well-honed communication skills, and advanced mathematics, science, and technical skills. Such competencies will prepare students, and our nation, for a world in which the following are a reality: economic competitiveness and jobs, global challenges, national security and diplomacy, and a diverse U.S. society. (p. 2)

The U.S. Department of Education (2017) subsequently released the Framework for Developing Global and Cultural Competencies to Advance Equity, Excellence, and Economic Competitiveness. These competencies fall under the broad domains of collaboration and communication, world and heritage languages, diverse perspectives, and civic and global engagement. The framework further defines globally and culturally competent individuals as those who are

- Proficient in at least two languages.
- Aware of differences that exist between cultures, open to diverse perspectives, and appreciative of insight gained through open cultural exchange.
- Critical and creative thinkers, who can apply understanding of diverse cultures, beliefs, economies, technology, and forms of government to work effectively in cross-cultural settings to address societal, environmental, or entrepreneurial challenges.
- Able to operate at a professional level in intercultural and international contexts and to continue to develop new skills and harness technology to support continued growth.

Supranational agencies, including the United Nations (UN) and the Organisation for Economic Co-operation and Development (OECD), also advocate for globally competent teaching and learning. The UN Sustainable Development Goals emphasize global citizenship as a crucial education outcome. For example, Target 4.7 reads as follows: "By 2030, ensure that all learners acquire the knowledge and skills needed to promote sustainable development, including, among others, through education for sustainable development and sustainable lifestyles, human rights, gender equality, promotion of a culture of peace and non-violence, global citizenship and appreciation of cultural diversity and of culture's contribution to sustainable development" (United Nations, 2019).

UNESCO—the United Nations Educational, Scientific, and Cultural Organization—defines global citizenship as inclusive of three core dimensions: 1) to acquire knowledge, understanding, and critical thinking about global, regional, national, and local issues and the interconnectedness and interdependency of different countries and population; 2) to have a sense of belonging to a common humanity, sharing values and responsibilities, empathy, solidarity, and respect for differences and diversity; and 3) to act effectively and responsibly at local, national, and global levels for a more peaceful and sustainable world (UNESCO, 2015).

The OECD is a supranational organization that promotes policies aimed at improving economic and social well-being around the world through 36 member countries. They administrate the Programme for International Student Assessment (PISA)—a yardstick that countries use to compare their education systems. In 2015, the PISA tested global competence among adolescents for the first time. The OECD (2018) defines global competence as consisting of four dimensions: 1) to examine local, global, and intercultural issues; 2) to understand and appreciate the perspectives and world views of others; 3) to engage in open, appropriate, and effective interactions with people from different cultures; and 4) to act for collective well-being and sustainable development. These dimensions closely mirror the four domains of global competence as set forth by the Asia Society and the Council of Chief State School Officers: investigate the world, recognize perspectives, communicate ideas, and take action (Mansilla & Jackson, 2011).

Closest to the core of teaching and learning has been a groundswell of education organizations that provide programs, instructional materials, tools, and professional development aimed at fostering global competence in students. The following is just a tiny sampling of those organizations:

- World Savvy, an education nonprofit founded in response to rising levels of xenophobia in the wake of the September 11 terrorist attacks, provides professional development for educators and project-based learning for K–12 students that "engages youth to learn, work, and thrive as responsible global citizens." To date, it has worked with hundreds of thousands of youth and thousands of educators. (www.world-savvy.org/world-savvy-classrooms)

- The Asia Society Center for Global Education has worked with schools as part of its International Studies School Network (ISSN) since 2003. The goal of the ISSN is to develop a school's capacity to prepare globally competent students through on-site coaching, resources and tools, global competence performance assessments, and networking activities. (https://asiasociety.org/international-studies-schools-network/our-services)

- Participate Learning partners with schools and districts to integrate global content into the classroom curriculum to bring in dual language immersion programs and to hire international teachers as cultural ambassadors and language instructors. With the mission of ensuring equitable and inclusive access to a globally focused education, the organization has served over 22,000 students and 3,000 local teachers in over 400 schools. (www.participatelearning.com)

- iEARN is an online platform that has connected more than 2 million youth and 50,000 educators throughout 140 countries as they participate in projects together that tackle real-world issues. (https://iearn.org/about)

- Empatico provides teachers of youth aged 6–11 with a free virtual exchange video platform that allows students to engage in learning activities with partner classrooms from different parts of the world. (https://empatico.org)

Collectively, organizations such as these are reaching millions of students worldwide and are posting positive effects on student engagement, achievement, and preparedness for life outside the school walls. Whether they use the nomenclature of *global education*, *global citizenship education*, or *globally competent teaching*, the goal of these organizations is the same: to cultivate global competence among students.

Global Learning on the Ground

What does global competence actually look like when applied to the "real world" of schools? It looks like high school students in Washington, DC collaborating with peers in Ghana over Skype as they brainstorm ways to apply STEM skills to create a water purification system that would serve the dual purpose of clearing lead from Washington's Anacostia River and pollutants such as pesticides and hospital waste from a lagoon used for fishing and irrigation in Uganda (Ingber, 2017). It looks like 4th grade students taking on the perspectives of American colonists, Native Americans, and British loyalists as they debate whether the colonies should declare independence from the British Empire. It looks like 1st grade students excited to tell their teacher how they are bringing trash-free lunches to school in an effort to reduce plastic pollution after reading a book on the topic as part of small reading group instruction.

Globally competent teaching facilitates the type of learning described in these scenarios—situations where students are actively engaged in and genuinely enjoying the learning process while simultaneously immersed in content-area instruction. Globally competent teaching is the dispositions, knowledge, and skills that teachers draw upon to instill global competence in students (Tichnor-Wagner, Parkhouse, Glazier, & Cain, 2019). Figure 1.2 lists and defines these 12 dispositions, knowledge, and skills.

Globally competent teaching brings the world into the classroom and takes the classroom into the world. At its core, globally competent teaching is an innovative instructional reform that shifts teaching and learning to be more authentic and student-centered. It becomes grounded in the real world and relevant to students' lives and interests. People, perspectives, and conditions are constantly in flux, as are the interests and experiences of students every year. Therefore, there is not one standard process or set curriculum for teaching global competence. Though this may seem daunting or overwhelming to be unable to easily follow a series of predetermined lesson plans for those who have never tackled global competence, it is ultimately liberating to have the flexibility to teach what matters to students in a way that feels right and will be most effective within your context.

That being said, there are guideposts that cut across the 12 globally competent teaching elements and that apply to teachers in any location, grade level, and subject area. These "signature pedagogies" of globally competent teaching include 1) integrating global issues and perspectives into everyday instruction; 2) authentically engaging students with issues, people, and places beyond their cultural affiliations and national borders; and 3) connecting their own experiences and those of their students to the curriculum (Tichnor-Wagner, Parkhouse, Glazier, & Cain, 2016).

As an example of how these signature pedagogies work together, a middle school math teacher in a small North Carolina city spent time in homestays in a village in Guatemala where families subsisted in large part from the food they grew in the gardens outside their homes. He shared his experience by having students conduct word problems that involved determining the largest possible area for a garden based on different amounts of fencing for the perimeter. As students applied curriculum-required math skills (e.g., calculating area and perimeter), the teacher engaged them in conversations about the differences in how kids around the world get food and do household chores, which prompted them to think deeply about the actions they take in their own homes regarding food acquisition and before- and afterschool activities.

As an example of how these signature pedagogies work together classroom observations of globally committed educators, my colleagues and I found that teachers shared their international experiences with students by decorating their classrooms with photos or artifacts from their travels and infusing knowledge gained from their experiences into lesson plans (Tichnor-Wagner et al., 2016). At a deeper level, by sharing their experiences first, teachers turned their classrooms into safe spaces where students felt comfortable opening up about their own cultural backgrounds and global experiences.

Figure 1.2 | Globally Competent Teaching Elements

Element	Definition
Dispositions	
Empathy and valuing multiple perspectives	Educators look inward to recognize the perspectives, stereotypes, and biases they hold and the beliefs and experiences that shaped them. Then they reflect on why their perspectives may differ from perspectives that diverge from their own.
Commitment to promoting equity worldwide	Educators strive toward the betterment of humanity and the planet as they learn about and tackle issues to promote equity, human rights, justice, peace, and sustainability.
Knowledge	
Understanding of global conditions and current events	Educators are aware of current issues relevant to the lives of their students, local community, country, and wider world.
Understanding of the ways that the world is interconnected	Educators understand how forces of globalization have connected our world economically, socially, culturally, politically, and ecologically and see themselves as part of the interdependent world.
Experiential understanding of multiple cultures	Educators have an awareness of their own cultural practices, values, and norms and seek opportunities to immerse themselves in cultures different from their own.
Understanding of intercultural communication	Educators have knowledge of verbal and nonverbal strategies to effectively interact with people from diverse cultures.

Skills	
Communicate in multiple languages	Educators are willing to learn new languages to connect with students and families from linguistically diverse backgrounds.
Create a classroom environment that values diversity and global engagement	Educators foster a community where students learn from and respect one another's diverse cultures and engage in discussions about global issues from a variety of perspectives.
Integrate learning experiences for students that promote content-aligned explorations of the world	Educators incorporate global learning into everyday instruction that clearly connects to the world beyond the classroom, using student-centered approaches.
Facilitate intercultural and international conversations that promote active listening, critical thinking, and perspective recognition	Educators provide ongoing opportunities for students to connect with individuals from diverse countries and cultures.
Develop local, national, and international partnerships that provide real-word contexts for global learning opportunities	Educators connect with schools, classrooms, or teachers in different countries or with local organizations (e.g., universities, cultural institutions, companies) to provide students with global perspectives as they engage in collaborative inquiries around shared learning goals.
Develop and use appropriate methods of inquiry to assess students' global competence development	Educators regularly use a mixture of authentic formal and informal assessments (e.g., classroom checklists, project rubrics, portfolios) to provide students with feedback and to inform their own globally oriented instruction.

Source: Adapted from *Becoming a Globally Competent Teacher* (Tichnor-Wagner, Parkhouse, Glazier, & Cain, 2019). Copyright 2019 by ASCD.

Simple actions such as these spark student curiosity about the world, make the content richer, and create a caring classroom environment.

These signature pedagogies are not hypothetical; they are borne out of real activities done in real classrooms with real educators—activities that are spiraled throughout the year. In other words, these educators have figured out how to embed global competence into the DNA of what and how they teach so they are consistently reinforcing outcomes such as feeling empathy, valuing diversity, understanding global conditions, communicating and collaborating across cultures, and problem solving.

Despite cross-sector cries that students need to develop skill sets that cover cognitive, social-emotional, and behavioral domains—and emerging evidence of the positive impact of globally competent teaching practices—globally competent teaching remains the exception in K–12 schools. A common challenge that teachers already doing this work have shared with me is operating as lone islands within their schools. These visionary teachers have lamented that even when their administrators applaud the work they are doing, they don't truly understand it and therefore do not adequately support it. It can't be left up to chance that students get opportunities to develop global competence. Systemic change is needed so every student, regardless of ZIP code, ability level, or random classroom assignment, has the opportunity to foster the skill set needed for a peaceful and prosperous future. As education historians Tyack and Cuban (1995) argued, "Teachers cannot do the job alone. They need resources of time and money, practical designs for change, and collegial support" (p. 10). This is where leadership comes in.

The Imperative for Globally Competent School Leadership

Leadership plays a central role in successfully implementing instructional reforms that target teaching and learning (Leithwood & Jantzi, 2006). School leaders directly and indirectly affect teacher behaviors and student outcomes through actions such as setting clear, learner-centered goals that the whole school works toward; allocating resources (e.g., time, materials, training, and staff) to meet those goals; and fostering a collaborative work environment (Desimone, 2002; Leithwood, Louis, Anderson, & Wahlstrom, 2004; Tichnor-Wagner, Harrison, & Cohen-Vogel, 2016). School leaders, therefore, are critical for starting and scaling global learning experiences for students.

What makes a school leader a true leader? Leadership does not arise out of a formal title. It comes from one's actions. A school leader can be anyone whose actions inspire others to act in ways that systemically change the educational experiences and outcomes of students—a teacher, school coordinator, curriculum specialist, school administrator, principal, district administrator, or superintendent. Globally competent school leaders take actions that inspire those around them to transform schools into relevant, engaging places of learning that prepare students for citizenship and jobs and to be agents of change in our diverse, interconnected world. These actions, whether bold or unassuming, positively affect school culture, the implementation of innovative reforms, and student learning (Tichnor-Wagner, 2019; Tichnor-Wagner & Manise, 2019).

An Implementation-Based Approach to Becoming a Globally Competent School Leader

Because leadership is born from action, this book takes an implementation-based approach to globally competent school leadership. As researcher Maureen McLaughlin (1990) observed after decades of research on school reforms, "Implementation dominates outcomes" (p. 12). It doesn't matter how inspiring your vision might be. Without concrete steps to transfer that vision into action, your vision will remain just that: words on a page in a policy document or a statement hanging on a wall.

Just as there is no single way to become a globally competent teacher (Parkhouse, Tichnor-Wagner, Glazier, & Cain, 2016), there is no single road to follow that will lead you to becoming a globally competent school leader. School leaders, even when coming from the same school district, have shared with me different motivations and journeys that brought them to embrace bringing the world into their schools. Some decided that their school community needed to reset how they perceived demographic shifts in the student population as being an asset to celebrate and not a challenge to endure.

Others began after a realization that their schools needed to better respond to market demands and the interests of students and families. Still others have always had a global focus in their personal and professional lives, having studied and worked overseas. There are, however, certain tools you can employ from wherever your journey began and toward wherever it may take you. A synthesis of decades of research examining policies and programs that lead to effective implementation of educational initiatives points to four domains of leadership actions to support you in successfully transforming your school into a place of global learning: alignment, will, resources, and capacity (see Figure 1.3).

Action 1: Align Aspirational Initiatives to Existing Ones

Schools are nested in a loosely coupled education system of community, district, state, and federal contexts. School leaders feel the push and pull of priorities and the demands of students, staff, families, district central office units, state government, and community groups—which are often not well coordinated and may even oppose one another (Datnow, Hubbard, & Mehan, 2002). Multiple improvement initiatives may be thrown at schools at the same time and from multiple directions: state policies, district reforms, federal programs, and vendors pitching instructional programs from outside the system (Honig & Hatch, 2004). School leaders are already charged with the task of creating coherence across varied and sometimes competing reform efforts (Hatch, 2001). Introducing one more thing on top of everything else may seem overwhelming. At the same time, it can be easy for school staff to ignore or abandon if they don't recognize how the work fits into the work already happening (Honig & Hatch, 2004).

School leaders overcome this hurdle by asking, "How does this new initiative meet the needs and mission we already have?" They identify overarching goals and strategies to meet these needs and engage in "bridging activities" to inform and enhance the implementation of their goals (Honig & Hatch, 2004). When implementers see compatibility between new initiatives and existing activities—and when they see compatibility across multiple levels of

Figure 1.3 | Leadership Action Domains

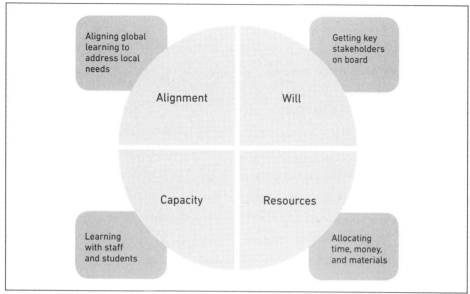

the education system—the new initiative will more likely be sustained and deepened (Coburn, 2003; Stringfield & Datnow, 2002). Therefore, globally competent leaders align global learning to address local needs and current policy constraints.

Action 2: Generate Will Across School Stakeholders

When there's a will, there's a way. When teachers, staff, parents, community members, and district-level decision makers believe in the value of a new initiative and show an eagerness and motivation to begin the work, they are likely to devote the time and energy to implement and support it. For changes to happen in a sustained way, the will of principals, district leaders, policy-makers, teacher education institutions, parents, and community members are all required. In other words, you need buy-in from those who will champion reforms using the power of the pulpit, formal and informal influencers within a school's network, and those actually tasked with implementation, such as, teachers and support staff. Buy-in and ownership among key stakeholders is often a determining factor in whether reforms are sustained (Coburn, 2003; Datnow et al., 2002; Newmann, Smith, & Allensworth, & Bryk, 2001). Therefore, globally competent school leaders identify and get key stakeholders on board and actively address concerns those stakeholders might have about bringing global education into the classroom.

Action 3: Wrangle Resources

Schools need money, materials, and time to see real changes to teaching practices (Hatch, 2001; Stringfield, Datnow, Ross, & Snively, 1998). Money can secure classroom supplies and additional staff to support implementation (e.g., instructional coaches). Time is essential for training school personnel in new ways of teaching, creating new lessons and units, and securing a place in the schedule for new initiatives to be taught. Though the availability of resources may be beyond the control of many school leaders (e.g., statewide funding streams, union-negotiated hours that schools can require teachers to attend, district-mandated schedule time blocks), leaders can, with a bit of foresight, effectively manage factors beyond their control (Hatch, 2001; Tichnor-Wagner et al., 2018). Therefore, globally competent school leaders work with what they have to figure out creative ways to dedicate time, money, and materials to global learning.

Action 4: Create Capacity

You can purchase the best curricular materials and newest technologies, but if teachers don't know how to use them, then it's wasted money. As multiple studies have concluded, teachers are the key component of the success of any effort aimed at fundamental school change (Desimone, 2002; McLaughlin, 1990). As such, investing in staff knowledge and skill-building around instructional reforms is imperative.

Teachers need opportunities for deeper learning on reforms that require changes to instructional practice. Without it, they might make unintended or marginal changes to practice—or not change their practice at all (Cohen & Hill, 2001; Spillane et al., 2002). Therefore, globally competent school leaders build capacity by providing ongoing professional learning opportunities for staff and join them and students on a schoolwide global learning journey.

Acting on all four of these domains will improve the likelihood that globally competent teaching and learning will take root and bloom. For example, if teachers have the will to implement but lack the capacity or resources, then implementation might not be possible. Alternatively, if teachers have the training but don't see how it aligns to competing programs the school is currently implementing or to high-stakes state tests, then implementation may be variable (Stringfield et al., 1998).

In addition, these four actions collectively reflect a top-and-bottom approach to implementation (Tichnor-Wagner et al., 2018), wherein school leaders adapt new programs and practices to fit their local contexts and needs of implementers on the ground. For example, school leaders look to see how global competence aligns with top-down policy initiatives and are able to clearly articulate that alignment while simultaneously building will among district leaders and policymakers who can champion—and fund—the cause from their positions of power. They can reallocate resources over which they have control toward global learning experiences. They also support globally competent teaching and learning from the bottom up, demonstrating an ability to align as they incorporate the needs and desires of teachers and students as they plan for global initiatives and an ability to build capacity as they allow teachers and students to design their own global learning experiences. An adaptive approach to leading instructional reforms is particularly salient to globally competent teaching and learning, an instructional reform that by design is meant to be adapted to the unique interests, needs, and location of each classroom and school.

Overview of the Book

This book describes the attributes that globally competent school leaders possess and how to leverage those attributes via the four effective implementation actions described above to systemically and sustainably support globally competent teaching and learning. Because the word *global* is interpreted by different people to mean vastly different things (Dolby & Rahman, 2008; Kirkwood, 2001), it is important to clarify how I use this term throughout this book. Globally competent teaching, global initiatives, and global programs all emphasize educational practices and structures that intentionally incorporate diverse perspectives into curriculum, instruction, and the culture of a school *and* that help reinforce the complexities of local, regional, national, and global identities, conditions, and connections. At the heart of global education is recognizing and valuing—rather than ignoring or rebuffing—the interconnectedness of our communities and selves to different people and places.

This book does not focus on understanding other countries through the lens of international or comparative education, which narrows the scope to studying policies, practices, and particularities within nation states (Dolby & Rahman, 2008). Although knowledge of different countries is an important component of global competence, as is knowledge sharing about educational practices in different parts of the world, it is but one piece contributing to a broader understanding of how we are all interconnected. At the same time, bringing global competence to a school is not a political act of preaching one-world government or encouraging students to trade in their national identities to become citizens of the world. To the contrary, global competence celebrates the local and national affiliations we have alongside our connection to a common humanity and gives students the tools to make their own informed decisions about the beliefs they ascribe to and the actions they take in local, national, and global arenas.

Chapter 2 presents seven tenets of globally competent educational leadership developed by ASCD and the Longview Foundation for the whitepaper *Globally Competent Educational Leadership: A Framework for Leading Schools in a Diverse, Interconnected World* (Tichnor-Wagner & Manise, 2019). These tenets were the result of a four-phase research project in which we analyzed pilot interviews of globally committed school leaders, conducted focus groups with 67 elementary and secondary school administrators from the United

States and abroad, and enlisted expert reviews from 39 individuals across the K–20 pipeline who have supported the implementation of global initiatives in schools—including school administrators, teachers, university professors, education association representatives, and individuals working in NGOs and state and federal government programs. These tenets are an aspirational set of skills for leaders to work toward, can be adapted to different contexts in different ways, and are aligned to general best educational practices. In short, they are a skillset that leaders can draw upon as they work toward implementing global initiatives.

Chapters 3–6 provide an in-depth examination of implementation actions you can take to lead schools in becoming globally relevant. Those actions are based on the four domains of alignment, will, resources, and capacity (illustrated in Figure 1.3 on page 21). Each of these chapters addresses barriers to implementation, solutions to overcoming those barriers, and examples of how school leaders have applied globally competent leadership tenets to these implementation actions. Chapter 3 examines how to align global initiatives with current policy trends and problems of practice that schools commonly contend with by building bridges between the local and global. Chapter 4 explores how to overcome political pushback to global teaching by building will among stakeholders who may be reticent to change because of policy incompatibility or antiglobal attitudes. Chapter 5 focuses on how to find the time and funding to spearhead global initiatives amid shrinking budgets and initiative overload. Chapter 6 examines how you can build capacity within yourself and your staff to implement global initiatives, even if you feel underqualified or ill prepared to lead such efforts.

The many examples of school leaders applying these tenets and taking actions toward leading global schools come from a compilation of interviews, observations, focus groups, and conversations I have conducted with a wide range of school and district administrators and teacher leaders that cut across different age cohorts, student populations, and geographic locations. Leaders I have interviewed and observed hail from the northeastern, southeastern, midwestern, and western United States; are in elementary, middle, high, K–8, and K–12 schools (predominately public and a handful of charter and private); are in urban, suburban, and rural communities; and work with student populations with varied economic, racial, linguistic, and cultural diversity. This 30,000-foot view that spans from elementary schools in rural North Carolina to middle schools in suburban Massachusetts to charter K–12 schools in Los Angeles has allowed me to draw upon the expertise and experience of an array of leaders who have infused global competence in varied ways. In doing so, I hope to illustrate how leading a global school can happen anywhere. (To protect the confidentiality of participants interviewed as part of research projects, I omit names of individuals and schools throughout the book.)

I also recognize that I am writing from a U.S.-centric perspective. I admit to the irony of writing a book about global competence from the lens of only one country. However, I do this intentionally. I ascribe to the notion that the global is grounded in the local (Peacock, 2007). What the world looks like depends on our perspective. What is foreign to one person is quotidian to another. It would be a near impossible task to write about how to align global competence to current priorities and build will in ways that attend to the intricacies of the political, social, and cultural landscapes that influence schools and school stakeholders' experiences in every country in the world, not to mention the scores of territories and indigenous and cultural groups within each country. As such, I encourage you to conduct this exercise from the location in which you are grounded while transferring that which is applicable to your context.

The concept of becoming a globally competent school leader may apply most directly to school administrators (e.g., principals, assistant principals, headmasters), yet it is also a clarion call to any and all educators ready and willing to begin the hard work of transforming schools into spaces for globally relevant and responsive learning. I have witnessed teachers, school coaches, curriculum specialists, district administrators, and superintendents lead global initiatives in schools. As I previously stated, actions—not titles— truly denote leadership.

This book focuses on globally competent school leadership, but the framework for its implementation can be transferred to other learning initiatives that—like globally competent teaching and learning—focus on real-world learning and cover social, emotional, and cognitive domains of development. A holistic approach to school leadership, one that grounds education in the complexities of the real world, is a need-to-have for all students, regardless of where in the world they call home. This book is an invitation to create possibilities for every student under your tutelage and lead to systemically level the playing field so all students can thrive in the world today and the future.

2

The Globally Competent
School Leader

---

*To live is to choose. But to choose well, you must know who you are and
what you stand for, where you want to go, and why you want to get there.*

Kofi Annan

As you walk into Pinewood International School, a public K–8 magnet school
in the rural southeast United States, you immediately get the feeling that you
are entering a global community of learners. National flags line the walkway
leading to the school entrance and, once inside, student work adorns the hallways: letters written to the principal by 7th grade students expressing their
commitments to making a difference in the world, sculptures made from
recycled materials decorating 1st grade doorways, and world maps on each
classroom door. Kindergarten students listen intently as their teachers give
directions in Spanish to line up outside the bathroom. The atrium displays
clocks with the local time and in Tegucigalpa, Nairobi, Manila, Auckland,
Kingston, Beijing, and London.

Almost none of the students attending Pinewood International have
ever left the United States. Indeed, a vast majority has never stepped outside
their county or state. Nevertheless, there is a palpable sense that these young
children are budding global citizens—with an awareness that they are a part
of a larger global community with diverse people, cultures, and languages.

They are growing a skillset that will help them navigate jobs in a global economy and find solutions to complex global issues, and they are developing an understanding that the actions they take can positively affect their local communities and the wider world.

Leadership has played a vital role in transforming Pinewood International from a low-performing school with a high student attrition rate into a place where students actively engage with one another, the curriculum, and their communities in ways that help them develop the skills they need for college, career, and citizenship in a diverse, interconnected world. School leaders built teacher capacity to turn a global vision for their students into a reality, requiring staff to participate in professional development and take on leadership roles with new global initiatives. They secured resources to support this learning, such as filling vacant staff positions with language teachers and providing time for teachers within and across grade levels to collaborate on global lessons and schoolwide global-themed investigations.

Pinewood International demonstrates that strong school leadership is vital in transforming a school into a place that fosters global competence among all students (Jackson, 2011; Wiley, 2013). Indeed, dedicated, supportive leadership is a central ingredient for schoolwide instructional reforms to be implemented in a meaningful, sustained way (McLaughlin, 1990). What, then, do school leaders do to support global competence development among teachers and students?

Simply put, globally competent school leaders engage in many of the same best practices of effective educational leaders. They create a shared mission and vision around student success, address equity and cultural responsiveness as they foster a community of care, build a professional community and capacity for educators, engage with families and community members, effectively manage resources, and have an eye toward school improvement (National Policy Board of Educational Administration, 2015). The main differentiator is that they do so through a global lens, intentionally focusing on global competence development as a way to support the academic, social, and emotional growth of all students.

ASCD and the Longview Foundation identified seven tenets of globally competent educational leadership that align with the Professional Standards for Educational Leaders (Tichnor-Wagner & Manise, 2019). Globally competent school leaders

- Facilitate, advocate, and enact a *shared mission and vision* of high-quality education that includes preparing students for life, work, and citizenship in a global society.
- Implement and support *curriculum, instruction, and assessment* that incorporate and promote the development of each student's global competence.
- Foster a *collaborative professional community* where administrators, teachers, support staff, students, and community members work together to build capacity around developing global competence for each student and staff member.
- *Connect and collaborate globally* to promote and support each student's academic success, well-being, and global competence development.
- *Advocate* for global competence and *engage* families, community members, and policymakers for support.
- *Manage school operations and resources* to support staff and student global competence development.
- Strive for *equity of access* to high-quality global learning opportunities for each student and *cultivate an inclusive, caring, and supportive school community* that values the cultural and linguistic diversity of each student.

These tenets paint a portrait of what globally competent school leadership looks like (see Figure 2.1). They set a gold standard toward which leaders who commit to making learning relevant for their students might aspire—in essence, the destination where they want to go. This chapter defines and illustrates each of these attributes in practice.

Figure 2.1 | Globally Competent Educational Leadership Tenets

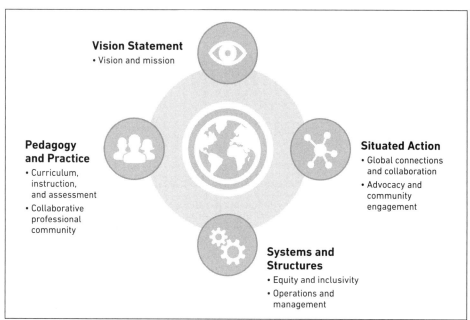

Facilitating a Shared Mission and Vision

Effective school leaders create and promote a mission and vision that support the whole child—that is, each student's academic success and social-emotional well-being—and around which all members of the school community rally. Preparing students for life, work, and citizenship in a global society is at the heart of that mission and vision for globally competent school leaders (Staudt, 2016; Stewart, 2010; Wiley, 2013).

Examples of globally oriented school visions and mission statements at elementary, middle, and high schools of leaders I have interviewed and observed include: "We will be innovative leaders working for positive change in our global community"; "Students will be well prepared for the next step in their education career as 21st century learners, responsible citizens, and productive members of a global society"; "Preparing students to excel in a diverse and ever-changing global society"; "Our school family will create powerful educational experiences that foster academic excellence, personal growth, and global citizenship"; "A learning community that prepares students to be responsible leaders in building a sustainable world"; "To navigate students toward being global lifelong learners."

Mission statements are only as good as the extent to which they come alive in the school. Globally competent leaders breathe life into a school's globally oriented mission in a number of ways. First, they bring multiple stakeholders together to collectively revise their shared vision and mission to include global learning. This helps foster commitment across the wider school community (Wiley, 2013). Leaders understand that the word *global* conjures up different connotations for different people and therefore get staff and the broader school community to agree on a common definition of what *global* means in their local setting.

Second, leaders connect the global competence mission to the needs and priorities of students and the school community. Often, schools may already have elements in place from which they can build. For example, some school leaders I interviewed built on the rich cultures represented within their student body, seeking to shed a positive light on the changing demographics in their community and utilizing that diversity as an entry point to learning about world cultures and languages. School leaders in military communities made natural connections between global competence and the international experiences inherent to their communities (i.e., moving between military bases around the world). Still other school leaders took advantage of district technology initiatives or schoolwide recycling and environmental programs to enhance their global curriculum. (Chapter 3 provides an in-depth examination of local-global connections.)

Third, leaders share the global mission, vision, and operational definition as widely as possible—announcing it on posters around the school, on the school's website and social media outlets, in school improvement plans and parent newsletters, during faculty meetings, and at schoolwide assemblies.

In communicating this out, they make visible the school's commitment to global learning and ensure it is lived out every day.

Fourth, school leaders engage in ongoing conversations with staff, students, and families about how global competence is incorporated into the school's everyday business. Discussions can take place through formal structures, such as global leadership teams composed of administrators, teachers, support staff, and community members who regularly meet to design and refine an implementation plan with clear action items, timelines, and delegation of responsibility. Conversations also include informal chats in the hallway, classroom, or cafeteria. Through such dialogues, leaders do not demand that subordinates act in one particular way. Instead, leaders actively listen to members of the community and make changes to how their school operationalizes the globally oriented mission based on the feedback they hear. In sum, they bring stakeholders together to develop a vision for global learning, devise a plan for implementation, and collectively lead the learning.

These follow-up actions help prevent the mission statement from becoming empty rhetoric or a series of isolated symbolic activities. A rural elementary school principal summarized the process this way: "As an administrator, my primary role is helping set and then model an expectation of global education." As demonstrated in the following sections, leaders model this expectation in how they support curriculum, instruction, and assessment; foster a collaborative professional community; forge their own global connections; advocate and engage with the community; manage operations and resources; and address issues of equity and inclusivity.

Supporting Curriculum, Instruction, and Assessment

Effective educational leaders implement and support systems of curriculum, instruction, and assessment that foster each child's academic and social-emotional development (National Policy Board of Educational Administration, 2015). *Globally competent* school leaders understand that globally competent teaching supports students' holistic success. When teachers integrate global competence by situating student learning in real-world contexts using inquiry-based instructional approaches, students become engaged in the learning process, are challenged to think critically and creatively, and learn to collaborate and communicate with people of diverse backgrounds and perspectives. Leaders recognize how important these student outcomes are and, as such, view global competence as a core pillar of education that enriches core subject areas, prepares students for college and careers, and addresses important aspects of social-emotional learning.

Leaders help classroom teachers incorporate global competence into curriculum, instruction, and assessment in a variety of ways. They provide scaffolds for global learning to be integrated across all content areas; schedule targeted courses, certificate programs, extracurricular activities, and special events; and emphasize formative and summative assessments that monitor students' global competence development and improve instruction (Stewart, 2010; Wiley, 2013).

Integrating Global Learning

Globally competent leaders support instruction that emphasizes integrating global competence and student diversity in all content areas and across all grade levels. When I ask school leaders about content-area instruction and global learning, words and phrases such as *mesh*, *blend*, and *the two go hand in hand* percolate to the surface. Simply put, they fundamentally believe that globally competent teaching should not be "one more thing." It is part and parcel of The Big Thing that education should drive toward: the holistic success of all students. Integrating global learning into the content areas feeds into equity of opportunity. If all teachers integrate global perspectives and content into their instruction, then all students will have access. Leaders support this work by recognizing what this integration looks like when done well and by providing training and support for teachers to succeed.

Leaders recognize that global integration into the content areas looks different depending on teachers' comfort level and experience. For teachers and schools just beginning this work, leaders understand that global integration is all about exposure to the world by plugging global content and perspectives into existing lessons: pointing out on a world map where a story or news article takes place, incorporating photos of volcanos around the world during a science lesson on volcanos, and selecting read-aloud picture books with protagonists reflective of diverse cultures. These examples don't require teachers to plan additional lessons; they just need to slightly tweak what they are already doing and when they are doing it.

As teachers become more adept at integrating global content, leaders help shift the emphasis toward utilizing student-centered learning strategies to investigate the world. Per the Globally Competent Learning Continuum (Tichnor-Wagner et al., 2019), as teachers become more proficient in implementing content-aligned explorations of the world, they plan units of inquiry around global issues that pique student interest and can be taught within the confines of specific subject areas. At the advanced level, it is the students leading the learning as they pursue interdisciplinary projects on issues they identify as important. More and more, students, teachers, and global education organizations are turning toward the Sustainable Development Goals as a great starting point for brainstorming real-world problems (Perrier, 2017). For example, how can we reduce the amount of lead in our water supply? Why do farmers in developing countries experience food insecurity? How can we disrupt the gender pay gap?

Project-based learning, design challenges, and service learning allow students to flex critical thinking and problem-solving muscles and authentically interact with local and global communities beyond the school walls. During project-based learning, students work on projects that are meaningful and relevant to their lives; collaborate with peers, experts, community members, businesses, and organizations; and publicly present their product to authentic audiences (High Quality Project Based Learning, n.d.). Design challenges prompt students to identify a problem to solve, conduct empathy interviews to understand the users' needs, define the problem from the users' point of view, ideate on possible solutions to the problem, create a prototype of the solution, and test the prototype to see if it solves the users' problem (Hasso Plattner Institute of Design at Stanford, n.d.). Service learning combines curricular objectives with societal needs as students work with a different community to combat issues the community faces.

For example, a principal in a Midwest global studies magnet school explained how project-based learning is the key vehicle for how his school incorporates global competence. The school created a global project plan that all teachers follow, which includes a connection to a global issue, entry events to engage students, and authentic audiences with which students can engage. For the first project of the year, all classrooms follow projects based around a schoolwide global theme. For the second project, teachers pick the issue individually or with their grade-level teams. Over time, teachers become comfortable moving from disciplinary to interdisciplinary approaches to help students investigate global issues.

Leaders facilitate implementation of global integration by providing teachers with frameworks and professional development resources. A number of organizations already exist that have comprehensive support systems for schoolwide global integration, including, for example, the International Baccalaureate's Primary Years Program, Middle Years Program, Diploma Program, Asia Society's International Studies Schools Network, World Savvy Partnerships, and Participate Learning.

Alternatively, leaders can facilitate a homegrown approach for integrating global learning that draws on the vision, interests, and expertise of staff. As one example of a homegrown approach, at Pinewood International School, every classroom researches, explores, presents, and takes action on a monthly theme (e.g., global leadership, arts around the world, human rights, the environment). As part of the environmental theme, the school planted a tree and students learned about Earth Day. Each grade level then took an in-depth look at the environment, researching a solution to a problem. First grade students explored how to reduce waste in the school cafeteria, whereas 7th grade students examined how to reduce the school's energy consumption and reliance on fossil fuels. The school leadership team supports this homegrown global learning approach by providing teachers with time to collectively brainstorm themes and activities during staff retreats and professional development days, which allows teachers across grade levels to collaborate.

Regardless of the route they choose, globally competent leaders continuously provide feedback for ongoing global integration by explicitly looking for connections in teachers' lesson plans, classroom observations, and walkthroughs. Though persistent, leaders are not prescriptive. They support a flexible curriculum that gives teachers autonomy to adapt lessons and units to students' interests and needs. They also provide scaffolds for teachers who are new to, unsure about, or overwhelmed by bringing global issues and perspectives into their content areas.

Global Courses, Programs, and Certificates

Leaders support the development of courses with an explicit global focus and accommodate those courses into the school schedule. For example, elementary school leaders have included world language and culture as a part of the rotating enrichment schedule that cycles with physical education, music, and art. Middle school leaders have used an extended homeroom period for global investigations and encouraged staff to develop globally oriented electives that build on their personal interests and expertise. High school leaders have offered global studies courses in addition to a robust world language curriculum.

Leaders have also adopted dual immersion language programs to support global competence goals. These programs strive to increase academic achievement in the content areas, develop bilingual and biliterate students, and promote cross-cultural competence by validating bicultural identities (Feinauer & Howard, 2014). Such programs teach the content areas in two languages and typically follow a 90:10 or 50:50 language split. They also ideally include an equal split of students who are native speakers of each language.

High school leaders can also have their respective schools participate in elective global certificate programs that award students who complete a certain sequence of courses and projects with an endorsement on their diploma. For example, the Illinois Global Scholar Certificate (www.illinoisglobalscholar

.org) requires students to take globally focused courses, participate in globally focused service learning and global collaboration, and complete a global capstone project. In Wisconsin, high school students can graduate with a Wisconsin Global Scholar distinction if they earn four credits in a world language, earn four credits in a course with global content, complete reflections on eight books with global content, participate in schoolwide global activities, and participate in global service learning (www.globalwisconsin. org/the-policy). Leaders in states without these certificates in place have also created their own. A high school principal in a Boston, Massachusetts, suburb created a Global Citizenship Certificate for upperclassmen that involved interdisciplinary academic coursework, community service, and international travel requirements. (The Global Education Certificate Toolkit, found at https://globaledcertificate.org, provides various models and case studies of what these certificates can look like.)

Extracurricular Programming

Leaders encourage global learning outside the classroom, as well. Extracurricular programs provide opportunities for students to expand their worldview and further explore their interests in ways that might not be possible within the time and content constraints of the classroom (Asia Society, 2009). These cover a gamut of activities, such as Model UN, world language clubs, multicultural clubs, international exchange trips, or even content-area tutoring that uses a global lens to engage students.

Special events, such as global passport nights, multicultural fairs, global-themed days, and international performances, are another way to support students' global learning. Leaders do not view one-off or annual events as a be-all-end-all of global learning. Rather, they use international fairs and special performances as a deliberate first step to drum up excitement around global learning and to tie special events back into the learning taking place in the classroom, carefully avoiding the "food, flags, and festivals" trap.

For example, at an elementary school in the rural southwest, each student is assigned a "vessel" from a specific region of the world. Once a month during Vessel Day, students conduct an in-depth exploration about their particular region (which is planned out by the school leadership team). An elementary school in a neighboring district has an annual Olympics style global field day in the spring as a culminating celebration of a year of integrated global learning. At the beginning of the school year, each teacher selects a country for his or her classroom to represent and incorporates that country into lessons throughout the year (e.g., selecting informational texts about that country, bringing in guest speakers from that country). During the global field day, classes participate in a parade of nations before competing in traditional field day activities.

Middle schools and high schools hold fairs where students present culminating projects or reports to their peers, school staff, parents, and community members. Providing opportunities for students to showcase their work to the wider school community has the added bonus of reinforcing to students and staff that global competence matters.

Assessing Global Competence

Leaders committed to global competence provide tools and time to help teachers assess it. Leaders recognize that global competence is a complex construct not easily measured by multiple choice tests and not quickly developed after a single lesson. Therefore, they encourage teachers to think about the particular aspects of global competence they want to measure (e.g., valuing multiple perspectives, understanding global interconnectedness, intercultural communication) and encourage teachers to use a range of formative (i.e., low-stakes, more frequent) and summative (i.e., higher-stakes, less frequent) assessments.

Formative assessment of students' global competence includes exit slips, observation notes or checklists, student work samples, and reflective journal entries. Summative assessments ask students to apply the knowledge and skills they've learned to real-world tasks. This may take the form of presentations, projects, essays, or portfolios (Tichnor-Wagner et al., 2019). For example, one K–12 charter school administrator shared how his whole school adopted a global competence digital portfolio, and each semester, students write a reflection on how they have grown as a global citizen. This approach was based on the Asia Society and CCSSO framework (Mansilla & Jackson, 2011) that has students investigate the world, recognize perspectives, communicate ideas, and take action and provide artifacts (e.g., classwork, projects) as evidence of their growth.

Few examples of assessments exist that measure K–12 students' global competence. Therefore, leaders provide time for staff to create them. (Because global competence is best taught when integrated into the content areas, you can also integrate global competence metrics into existing project rubrics.) A few resources that can help staff reflect on how to measure global competence in their classrooms include the following:

- **The Globally Competent Learning Continuum.** Specifically, Element 12—developing and using appropriate methods of inquiry to assess global competence development—provides a definition and links to resources for global competence assessment. (https://globallearning. ascd.org)
- **The PISA 2018 Global Competence Framework.** The website includes a definition and breakdown of the knowledge, skills, and dispositions that comprise global competence and a sample questionnaire for the triannual survey of 15-year-old students. (www.oecd.org/pisa/ pisa-2018-global-competence.htm)
- **Asia Society Global Competence Outcomes and Rubrics.** Asia Society's Graduation Performance System provides a set of global competence performance outcomes for elementary, middle, and high school grades in leadership, math, science, art, social studies, and language arts. (https:// asiasociety.org/education/global-competence-outcomes-and-rubrics)

Fostering a Collaborative Professional Community

Teachers need time and resources to develop the professional capacity to effectively incorporate global and cultural perspectives into their classrooms.

Anthony Jackson (2011) writes, "No matter how passionate they are about global learning, teachers cannot teach what they do not know. Teachers need professional development opportunities to update their ability to integrate meaningful global content and develop students' global competence" (p. 68). As such, globally competent school leaders prioritize global competence as a key feature of staff professional learning, and they do so in a way that encourages collaboration toward building collective capacity.

Not all professional learning opportunities are created equal when it comes to building teacher capacity and improving student outcomes. Effective professional learning scaffolds teacher learning, focuses on content and pedagogy, uses hands-on approaches that allow for teachers to adapt content to fit the needs of their students, and is sustained over time (Borko, 2004; Borko, Mayfield, Marion, Flexer, & Cumbo, 1997; Cohen & Hill, 2001; Garet, Porter, Desimone, Birman, & Yoon, 2001; Guskey, 2002, 2003). Effective professional learning for global competence follows these same principles. Leaders don't have to facilitate professional development sessions to actively support staff professional learning, but they can identify instructional coaches or professional development providers best suited to do so. Leaders also provide feedback on global integration after classroom observations and walkthroughs, add global connections to lesson plan templates, consistently share ideas and resources via weekly email blasts, and identify additional professional development offerings (e.g., free webinars, workshops) for staff to attend.

Leaders also encourage teachers to pursue nontraditional professional development for global learning, such as microcredentials and immersion experiences. Microcredentials are personalized, on-demand professional learning experiences wherein teachers submit evidence of competency on a specific, "bite-sized" topic; receive timely feedback and a digital badge from a reviewer; and can then share that badge with colleagues and administrators (Center for Teaching Quality & Digital Promise, 2016). Bloomboard and Digital Promise issue stacks of microcredentials, each of which focuses on a different aspect of global competence.

Teacher exchange programs that immerse teachers in a new country or culture can increase global competence development, particularly in the areas of empathy, valuing of diverse perspectives, knowledge of global conditions and cultures, intercultural communication skills, awareness of students' diverse backgrounds and needs, and ability to incorporate multicultural and global perspectives into lessons and units (Cushner & Brennan, 2007; DeVillar & Jiang, 2012; Mahon, 2010; Zong, 2009). I have observed leaders support immersion opportunities in numerous ways: directly forging partnerships with a district in a different country that involved annual teacher exchanges, issuing stamps of approval for teachers who independently seek out short-term international teaching experiences, and granting a sabbatical for teachers seeking semester-long immersion experiences. For example, the Fulbright Distinguished Awards in Teaching program ranges from two to six weeks, whereas the semester research program is three to six months (U.S. Department of State, 2019).

Finally, leaders foster a collaborative culture wherein administrators, teachers, support staff, students, and community members work together to develop global competence. To do so, leaders create time and space for staff to collaborate. Through structures such as committees, shared planning time, and staff retreats, they provide opportunities for teams of teachers to generate ideas for, plan, and implement schoolwide global initiatives. They allow teachers to coach peers on how to integrate global concepts into the curriculum, organize sister school collaborations and global festivals, and attend conferences and summits to pick up innovative ideas. Leaders also ask students to generate ideas for schoolwide global events or service projects. This shared sense of ownership across the school community mitigates the risk of global initiatives grinding to a halt if the one key principal or teacher driving the work leaves.

One elementary school principal in a small southeastern city used the International Baccalaureate Primary Years Program framework to build collective school capacity around global competence development. She spent five years slowly developing staff capacity to globalize instruction. During the summer, she led staff through workshops in which they studied the IB learner profile and attitudes and laid out the state standard course of study to determine where global content naturally fit. Throughout the school year, teachers used grade-level planning time to collaboratively develop units that incorporate global themes and are aligned to state standards. In addition, she allocated funds for teachers to attend additional IB workshops on globalizing instruction. She explained, "Taking smaller steps and going more in depth with your learning, both as a staff and as a student, is much better than just trying to hurry up and get it done."

Connecting and Collaborating Globally

Leaders make local and global connections to promote and support each student's academic success, social and emotional well-being, and global competence development. Educational leaders across international divides have much to learn from one another. Professors Gaetane Jean-Marie, Anthony Normore, and Jeffrey Brooks (2009) implore us, "Imagine a world in which school leaders look not only to their peers in a neighboring school district or even another U.S. city for ideas and solutions that might help their students, but to a global community of leaders who understand that the success of the local should be informed by and contribute to the success of students around the globe" (p. 18). Global connections and collaborations born out of international travel and exchange, school partnerships, and global professional learning networks can turn that vision into a reality.

International Travel and Exchange

Overseas travel is the quintessential global learning experience, one of the first things that comes to mind when thinking of global education. When possible, leaders seek opportunities to participate in international travel that involves 1) in-depth learning about a country's culture, history, geography, government, and education systems, and 2) avenues for building relationships with educators from that region. When signing up for an international program, leaders should look for those that provide more than surface-level, touristy encounters

(Alfaro & Quezada, 2010). Programs should provide opportunities for leaders to go on school visits, meet with educators to learn new practices from around the world, and authentically connect with local residents.

An elementary school principal who participated in international programs to Mexico and Japan commented, "As adults, having those opportunities to travel abroad—not just to look at the beautiful scenery but to talk to people about important previous and current global events—increases our worldview. That's important if we're going to be global educators and do a good job of helping our children have a global perspective." Leaders can also host international colleagues at their school or in their district. This might involve giving tours of your school, providing opportunities for your guests to give talks or workshops about education in their country, or opening up your home for meals and accommodation.

The relationships leaders form when traveling overseas or hosting international colleagues allows for profound personal growth and can lead to many tangible and unexpected benefits for their entire school.

School Partnerships

One elementary school principal and a small team of teachers went on a two-week immersion trip to Mexico where they connected with a local principal to form a sister school partnership focused on two goals: building students' intercultural communication skills and enhancing curricular studies. When they returned, the principal infused the partnership into all facets of students' school experience. Regular Skype sessions with the sister school were incorporated into the weekly schoolwide morning meeting, which helped build a sense of community between the two schools and helped students develop intercultural communication skills. The partnership created authentic opportunities for classroom teachers to delve deeper into their curriculum as well. For example, a 4th grade class presented to and fielded questions from their counterparts in Mexico via Skype for a research project on Native American cultures; and a 3rd grade class conducted a joint inquiry on constellations and planets, whereby students compared the night sky in their two locations using telescopes the principal received through a grant.

Partnerships with a school in another country can take many different forms: teacher and student exchanges, collaborative student projects aligned to content-area standards, school-to-school video chats, or pen pal correspondences. Schools should mold partnerships to best fit their mission and needs. For example, an elementary school with an environmental theme in North Carolina virtually partnered with a school in Finland. Students in both schools conducted a series of joint projects related to recycling, including creating arts and crafts for one another out of recycled materials. Another elementary school principal in that district committed to providing her teachers with globally focused professional development, set up a partnership with a school in Belize, and helped facilitate annual teacher exchanges. She explained her rationale, "For teachers to be global educators, they have to have an experience . . . whether that's collaborating with an international teacher colleague or actually having an international experience themselves."

Global Professional Learning Networks

Leaders form and maintain relationships with colleagues from their region or country and from around the world to widen their professional learning networks (Lindsay, 2016; Staudt, 2016). They meet new colleagues through conferences, workshops, and word-of-mouth from neighboring school districts, and they stay in touch with those colleagues to learn how to integrate global content; how to initiate programs, professional development offerings, and global initiatives; and how colleagues in different contexts respond to challenges related to students' academics, health, and social well-being.

Leaders also broaden their network without boarding an airplane or getting in a car, thanks to online professional learning networks and communities of practice, which can be accessed through various mediums, such as Twitter, Facebook, webinars, online TeachMeets, and Google Hangouts (Lindsay, 2016). These platforms can also reinforce and sustain connections made during international travel. As one assistant principal shared, "What's amazing is that when you start really embracing global education, you get connections from places you wouldn't even dream of. They have connections, and then their connections become your connections. What's amazing is that the kids can see these connections."

This assistant principal used the global connections she created and maintained through Twitter and Facebook to enhance student curriculum. She considers the many teachers she met who have lived in other countries to be vital resources for her school. For example, when a teacher shared with her an upcoming unit on volcanos, she immediately remembered a colleague who taught near a volcano in Puebla, Mexico. She contacted that colleague and connected with her classroom over video chat, which allowed students to ask questions about the volcano. She shared, "The kids learned that they had signals for when they can't go outside because ashes were falling. You wouldn't get that from a textbook. All you get from a textbook is whether the volcano is dormant or not and the type it is. You don't learn how to live beside a volcano. That's why connections are vital for global education."

Advocating and Engaging the Community

Leaders advocate for global competence and engage families, the community, and policymakers for support. They explain the importance of global competence to various stakeholders, including school staff, students, parents, district administrators, school board members, community members, and state policymakers (Lindsay, 2016; Staudt, 2016). Advocacy activities involve educating teachers and parents about how global learning benefits student outcomes in school and beyond; inviting parents, district leadership, and community members to events that showcase student work; presenting students' projects and lessons to school boards; persistently pitching proposals for global programs to district leadership; serving on district, state, and national task forces on global education; serving on district or state commissions that examine global competence; and petitioning policymakers to fund global programs.

In addition to advocacy outreach, leaders seek input from families and community members as they pilot and refine global initiatives. I have seen this done in numerous ways: parent surveys, town hall–style meetings that provide space for parents' and community members' questions to be answered, and informal conversations. For example, one rural elementary school principal surveyed parents to gauge interest before initiating a Spanish immersion program, knowing that some community members might be wary of teaching students in another language. Once the program got off the ground, the principal regularly checked in with the parents of students who enrolled. This opened his eyes to parents' fears that they couldn't help their children with homework because they didn't know the language, and it prompted the school leadership team to devise ways to provide Spanish resources to English-speaking parents.

When engaged, parents can be tremendous resources for students' global learning experiences. Whether parents have immigrated from another country, work for a company that conducts international business, or both, leaders welcome them to share their experiences with students as guest speakers during schoolwide events or in specific classrooms studying a relevant topic or region (Muller, 2012).

Globally competent leaders also reach out to local community organizations, such as businesses, nonprofits, and international groups, to garner support for global learning (Stewart, 2010). Local businesses can serve as strong allies and advocates for global learning. Because many business associations have a powerful voice in local and state government, business leaders can help education leaders garner political support by sharing their need for a globally competent workforce. Furthermore, businesses can help sponsor programs—from afterschool extracurriculars to student internships to exchange programs. Nonprofits with a global or cultural focus may be able to provide professional development to staff, consult on the direction of the school's global mission, provide speakers for schoolwide assemblies, or serve as a community partner for field trips or service-learning projects.

Local colleges and universities can also be a great resource, as they might offer travel exchange programs for administrators and teachers, virtual exchange programs that connect K–12 classrooms to the wider world, grant-writing assistance to jumpstart global programs, and Title VI centers that offer classroom resources for specific regions of the world.

Managing Operations and Resources

Leaders manage school operations and resources to support global competence development among teachers and students. They allocate resources toward globally oriented professional development, instructional materials, programming, and staff. To sustain relevant initiatives, particularly when school budgets are tight, leaders find ways to fund new programs with existing monies, often making the pertinent decisions with school staff.

For example, they focus mandatory staff training time on global competence; set aside professional development funds to send teachers to conferences, seminars, and other programs with global content; and offer sabbaticals to teachers who travel abroad for professional teaching, research, and learning. When new staff positions open up, leaders prioritize hiring international teachers, world language teachers, and teachers who demonstrate a commitment to global learning. As one elementary school principal in the southeast explained, "I can choose to either get a local teacher or to get an international teacher, but [the district is] not giving me an extra teacher spot, an extra salary to fill that. That's an internal thing that we decide to do as a school." Earmarking time or money for global competence sends a message that global learning is an important priority worthy of investment.

In addition to reallocating existing funds, leaders seek out new fiscal sources to support global learning—from local foundation grants to in-kind contributions from businesses to schoolwide fundraisers. They recognize that state and district budgets are not the only way to receive a deposit. Philanthropy and crowdsourcing are viable ways to make global learning a reality.

Finally, leaders review and amend school and district policies to ensure they support global learning opportunities. For example, leaders check to see if their district has a policy on travel abroad for students. If the district does not allow it, then they advocate for changing it. If the district has no policy in place, then they might write language that sets the parameters for those valuable learning experiences to occur.

Striving for Equity and Inclusivity

Undergirding all these tenets is a leader's unwavering commitment to equity and inclusivity. Globally competent leaders ensure that every student, regardless of ability level, race, ethnicity, home language, or poverty level, has equitable access to global learning opportunities. By equity, I mean providing to students according to their needs so they all have the same opportunity to thrive. This is not the same as equality. Equal access would distribute global learning opportunities exactly the same to all students, no matter their background. Equitable access means that some students receive more supports to finish in the same place as their peers (Mann, 2014; Tichnor-Wagner & Manise, 2019). Leaders recognize this important distinction. They also understand that students, staff, and they are entangled in a web of cultural, regional, national, and global affiliations, and they honor the multifaceted and complex identities that make up who we are (Banks, 2008).

Providing Access

The U.S. Department of Education (2012) argued, "Global competencies are not a luxury for a select few, but rather, are essential skills for all individuals" (p. 5). This is because global and cross-cultural competence is a skill set that employers seek among potential employees (Committee for Economic Development, 2006; Sodexo, 2015; World Economic Forum, 2018), and global learning opens students' eyes to a world of possibilities for economic security and personal fulfillment. Failing to provide students with the opportunity to develop global and cross-cultural competence shuts doors that could lead toward personal and professional success and happiness.

To provide equitable access, leaders train *every* teacher to integrate global competence into his or her teaching so that all students, regardless of their class schedule, will have exposure to the knowledge, skills, and dispositions required of a robust 21st century workforce. Making a world language, such as Spanish or Mandarin Chinese, a rotating elective alongside art, music, and PE ensures that each student has exposure to a new language and the cognitive and social-emotional benefits that go along with that.

Equity is also about providing more for those who don't have enough. Leaders tear down financial roadblocks by setting up foundations and fundraising plans so international travel and fundraising plans are free to those who cannot afford it. They give priority to students and staff who have yet to travel abroad when the school sponsors a new exchange. They eliminate GPA requirements so more students can enroll in global citizenship certificate programs. They offer world language courses for heritage speakers, which are designed for students with proficiency in or a cultural connection to a language other than English. When selecting dual immersion programs, leaders focus on a language spoken by many of their nonnative English speakers, and they are conscious not to privilege the experience of English-dominant students.

Including and Affirming All Students

Leaders also cultivate an inclusive, caring, and supportive school community that values the cultural and linguistic diversity of each student. They view schools as microcosms of the diverse world in which we live and see student diversity as an asset to the school community—a foundation upon which all students and staff can develop a global perspective. Accordingly, they act in ways that authentically welcome and incorporate the cultures, languages, and perspectives of students and students' families. Leaders work hard so students from diverse backgrounds see their cultures folded into the fabric of the school, teachers incorporate students' varied backgrounds and identities into daily learning (Gay, 2010; Paris, 2012), and service delivery accommodates the needs of culturally and linguistically diverse learners (Muller, 2012; Rodberg, 2016).

Leaders foster a welcoming environment by cultivating caring relationships with students and families from all backgrounds, incorporating students' home languages into parent communications and instructional resources, and providing space in schoolwide décor and activities for children to see themselves (Gay, 2010; Johnson, 2007). To actively tap into students' rich perspectives, experiences, and backgrounds as a foundation for learning, leaders provide explicit training for culturally responsive teaching and culturally sustaining teaching pedagogies in the classroom. Culturally responsive teaching relates all aspects of learning to students' cultural backgrounds (Gay, 2010). Culturally sustaining pedagogy takes this a step further, focusing on sustaining cultural and linguistic pluralism as an integral part of school transformation (Paris, 2012). Using students' culture as a vehicle for learning is an issue of equity unto itself. Research shows that culturally responsive practices help students historically marginalized from the curriculum understand and engage in learning and promote positive identity formation (Gay, 2010; Ladson-Billings, 1995; Paris, 2012).

Leaders also take a programmatic approach to meeting the needs of culturally and linguistically diverse learners. Take dual immersion programs, for example, whose goal is to produce bilingual, bicultural, and culturally competent students. Another example is Spanish for Spanish Speakers classes, which help students master academic and professional language in their native tongue. The very act of teaching academic content in students' home language shows them that the school values their heritage, helps students foster a positive cultural identity, and increases academic achievement in the content areas. Leaders might also create newcomer centers or start family literacy programs to help recent immigrants acclimate to the new language and educational norms of their new home while sustaining their own heritage, language, and culture.

Leaders also model culturally responsive behavior with school staff, hiring high-quality teachers who represent and value diverse cultural and linguistic backgrounds and treating the varied cultural, linguistic, and national backgrounds of teachers as assets to the school community. An elementary principal emphasized how staff from diverse backgrounds helps cultivate global competence: "There is nothing better to promote the global perspective than to have people from around the globe in your school. That has helped my staff. You can go to all the professional development you want to, but when you work day in and day out with people who are from another country, then you really begin to internalize the importance of imparting that global perspective to all of your children." Whether interacting with students, families, or staff, leaders create an environment where everyone feels valued, respected, and safe to express their opinions and perspectives.

In sum, globally competent school leaders apply best practices of leadership with a global orientation to transform education to reflect and respond to our interconnected, diverse world. Combined, these seven tenets show that globally competent school leaders shift the mindset, culture, and organizational structures of their school community to one that prepares each student for life and work in a global society. These tenets can be used to align the local and global, build will, wrangle resources, and build capacity—all of which answer this crucial question: How do we turn our schools into places that graduate students ready for the world?

Reflection and Action

Review and reflect on the seven tenets of globally competent educational leadership (see Figure 2.2).

Figure 2.2 | Globally Competent Educational Leadership Reflective Questions

Tenet	Reflective Questions
Shared Mission and Vision	Do I . . . • Work with staff and stakeholders to conceptualize what global competence means for our school community? • Communicate this mission? • Identify existing programs and current gaps? • Measure and report progress in meeting implementation and student outcome metrics of our global mission?

Tenet	Reflective Questions
Curriculum, Instruction, and Assessment	Do I . . . • Align current standards, curriculum maps, and assessments with global competence outcomes? • Support staff in using existing courses across all subject areas to embed global perspectives and themes? • Support staff and students in developing and implementing disciplinary and interdisciplinary project-based units that focus on global topics?
Collaborative Professional Community	Do I . . . • Share information on global learning opportunities and resources with staff? • Block out shared planning time for staff within and across departments to share best practices for integrating global learning? • Provide job-embedded professional learning around global competence? • Provide feedback on global lessons? • Allow staff, students, and administrators to lead global learning?
Global Connections and Collaborations	Do I . . . • Engage in professional networks with a global reach? • Develop partnerships with schools in other regions and countries? • Participate in local, national, and international cross-cultural exchanges, either face to face or virtually?
Advocacy and Engagement	Do I . . . • Reach out to local businesses, universities, community organizations, and cultural initiatives that might support global learning? • Engage families as partners in global learning? • Promote the importance of global learning to key stakeholders in a variety of ways?
Operations and Resource Management	Do I . . . • Allocate existing resources toward global learning? • Seek out new resources that support global learning? • Review and revise school and district policies to support global learning?

continued

Figure 2.2 | Globally Competent Educational Leadership Reflective Questions (*continued*)

Tenet	Reflective Questions
Equity and Inclusivity	Do I . . . • Ensure that each student has equitable access to global learning opportunities? • Seek to hire staff with diverse backgrounds and experiences? • Create space to engage with staff in critical self-reflection to examine personal perceptions of diversity and biases? • Create space for ongoing dialogue with families and community members that allows diverse perspectives to be heard? • Leverage the cultural diversity of students in classroom activities, clubs, and electives?

Source: From *Globally Competent Educational Leadership: A Framework for Leading Schools in a Diverse, Interconnected World,* by A. Tichnor-Wagner and J. Manise, 2019, Alexandria, VA: ASCD. Copyright 2019 by ASCD and Longview Foundation. Adapted with permission.

1. Of the seven tenets of globally competent educational leadership, which ones are your greatest strengths? Why?

2. In which tenets do you need the most improvement? Why?

3. What barriers are preventing you from doing these things? What do you have in your control to overcome these barriers?

3

Starting from Within

Our ambitions must be broad enough to include the aspirations and needs of others, for their sakes and for our own.

Cesar Chavez

Pause for a moment to situate yourself. Where are your feet planted? What do you see around you? Now turn your gaze inward. How do you identify yourself? With what ethnic, racial, religious, social, and political groups do you identify? What issues matter to you the most?

What you see and feel may appear immediately local and personal, yet this is exactly where the journey of global learning begins. As you begin to zoom out—your school is in a neighborhood, city or town, county, state, region, country, continent—and map out the hundreds, thousands, millions, or even billions of people who share the same identity markers, you begin to recognize that you are but a piece of a much larger global puzzle. The same goes for each of your students and staff members.

Upon further reflection, you may find that you, your students, and your staff already have connections to people and places around the world and already partake in activities that, intentionally or not, strengthen those connections. At the same time, you might also find that, even if global connections are present, they are overshadowed by competing priorities: college and career readiness, new teacher evaluations, high student drop-out rates, persistent achievement gaps, school closures, and budget deficits. The list goes on and on. Such competing priorities and urgent needs may appear to pose a barrier to global learning. Therefore, aligning global competence with what your school is already doing can help address immediate local concerns.

Barrier: Why Focus on Global Learning When There Are So Many Local Issues to Contend With?

School leaders today face an unrelenting number of challenges, including ensuring that students perform well on standardized tests; eliminating achievement gaps; helping English language learners adjust to a new language and culture; meeting the social, emotional, and physical needs of students who live in poverty or experience traumatic events; implementing new teacher evaluations; and grappling with state and federal budget cuts while seeking coherence between constantly changing policy mandates. From a 30,000-foot view, the simple act of getting kids into a classroom remains an issue of global concern. Worldwide, more than 250 million (or one in every five) school-aged children do not attend school, for reasons ranging from poverty, lack of access to classrooms, gender discrimination, conflict, and natural disasters (United Nations, 2018). In the United States, where school attendance is compulsory, over 6.5 million students are chronically absent, meaning they miss three or more weeks of school a year (Attendance Works & Johns Hopkins University, 2016).

School staff might quickly conclude that addressing immediate issues such as these takes precedence. After all, if we can't get students to be physically present in the classroom, does it even matter what we teach? If we don't meet students' basic health and safety needs, will they be able to focus on solving grander global challenges? If my evaluation is based on student test score performance, shouldn't that be my focus? As one school superintendent explained to me, global education is nobody's emergency. Therefore, it takes a back seat to other crises—not to mention job requirements.

Global competence is not a panacea for these multifaceted issues. It will not ameliorate poverty, nor will it prevent budget shortfalls. Nevertheless, when introduced in the right way, a schoolwide focus on global learning can help you address—and possibly solve—any number of short-term and long-term challenges.

Solution: Build Bridges Between the Local and Global

Overcoming the obstacle of competing local concerns begins with the simple understanding that your local school community and the challenges it faces are both part of the wider world. Global competence is glocal. The word *glocal* refers to the dynamic interplay of local and global forces (Robertson, 1995). Global conditions have local ramifications, and when we take small actions to improve local conditions, those actions can make a difference on a much grander scale. When you look at the world through a glocal lens, you begin to recognize that actions, conditions, and events that occur in your own back-yard have ripple effects around the world, and what happens in other parts of the world can also shape the immediate issues with which you are contending. Leaders who can make these connections and align global competence to existing school, district, and state priorities are likely to see school stakeholders embrace global initiatives.

Global competence should complement—not compete with—pressing issues you face. Fostering an understanding of the world doesn't have to supplant the need for students to understand the standard course of study, themselves, and their communities. Indeed, the content areas are a powerful vehicle through which global competence can be fostered (Tichnor-Wagner et al., 2019). Furthermore, cultural, national, and global identifications and experiences are interactive and interrelated, and they need to be equally cultivated within students to build an affirmative identity and sense of belonging (Banks, 2008). As such, there is added value in addressing students' overlapping and intersecting layers of self, community, country, and world.

The term *glocal* and the phrase *think globally, act locally* remind us that global concerns should not replace local concerns. Instead, the choice to "glocalize" education recognizes that schools are not immune to the increased speed and spread of people, goods, services, ideas, and politics across borders and can do so in the service of existing community concerns. What follows are examples (and certainly not an exhaustive list!) of local education issues with potential glocal learning remedies.

Student Achievement

Student achievement is a perennial concern. Since the 1990s, education policies around the world have attached stringent accountability demands to student test scores, particularly in post-industrial nations responding to the new knowledge economy (Ball, 1998). The so-called global education reform movement has prioritized numeracy and literacy, standards, prescribed curriculum, aligned assessments, and high-stakes accountability (Sahlberg, 2006). Consequently, this has shifted the primary focus of schools to raising student proficiency in tested subject areas.

For example, in the United States, No Child Left Behind—the 2001 reauthorization of the Elementary and Secondary School Act—penalized principals and schools who did not meet adequate yearly progress on state reading and math exams. Punitive measures included giving parents the option to leave the school, replacing staff who contributed to the school's low performance, decreasing the school's authority management, restructuring the school as a charter school, replacing a majority of staff, and turning school operations over to the state or a private company. Although the Every Student Succeeds Act, which replaced No Child Left Behind in the 2015 Elementary and Secondary School Act reauthorization, takes a step back from such a narrow focus on student achievement by adding nonacademic measures to state accountability plans, it still requires standardized testing in reading, math, and science. Furthermore, states continue to incorporate student test scores as part of teacher and administrator evaluations, thus putting continued pressure on leaders to focus on student achievement in tested subject areas.

Adding to the pressure leaders face in raising test scores, state and national assessment data reveal persistent achievement gaps based on income and race. Cultural biases are embedded in assessments (Greenfield, 1997), and research suggests that such biases may contribute to lower performance among non-white, less-affluent subgroups of students (Walton & Spencer, 2009). However, as long as standardized tests are benchmarks for student success—and in many cases gatekeepers to rigorous coursework, diplomas, and higher education enrollment—educators concerned about equitable outcomes for all students will understandably focus their energies on closing that gap. Because global competence is not a part of required testing, it is easy to push it to the periphery. A skeptic might ask how we can expect students to learn about the world if they haven't mastered reading or basic math skills. Aren't we doing our students a disservice if we don't first teach them the fundamental building blocks and then prepare them for the tests that will directly affect their future?

Test-based accountability does not seem to be disappearing anytime soon. However, there has been a recent push away from testing rote skills to testing the skills that a global competence–infused education requires. The Common Core State Standards, adopted by 42 states and the District of Columbia, emphasize communication skills, critical thinking, problem solving, real-world application, and an understanding of other perspectives and cultures—all of which are key competencies students need to succeed in a diverse, interconnected world.

In addition, coalitions of diverse stakeholders are fiercely advocating for a redefinition of student success that incorporates cognitive, social, and emotional development. For example, the culminating report of the Aspen Institute National Commission on Social, Emotional, and Academic Development (2019)—whose commission members included leaders from education, research, policy, business, and the military alongside youth and parents—recommended that schools broaden the definition of student success to include the whole child, transform learning settings to become physically and emotionally safe for all students, and change instruction to intentionally cultivate social, emotional, and cognitive skills in individual classrooms and across schoolwide practices. The OECD Learning Framework for 2030, which provides policy recommendations to 36 member nations, incorporates a broad set of knowledge, dispositions, attitudes, and values in its broad definition of the competencies students will need to be future-ready. This includes disciplinary, interdisciplinary, epistemic, and procedural knowledge; cognitive and metacognitive, social and emotional, and physical and practice skills; and personal, local, societal, and global attitudes and values (OECD, 2018). ASCD, an education association with over 100,000 members, including teachers, school and district administrators, superintendents, and teacher educators, released *The Learning Compact Renewed: Whole Child for the Whole World* (2019) to restate their commitment to a systems-wide approach for educating the whole child so every student is healthy, safe, engaged, supported, and challenged.

However, these recommendations for a more holistic education have yet to translate from paper to accountability policy. Part of your role as a globally competent school leader is to make explicit the connections between global competence and the measures of success that schools are currently held accountable for. An elementary school principal whose school was first beginning to integrate global concepts across the curriculum explained,

> Working in a school where students are underperforming and coming from homes where they have a lot of needs, the teachers are overwhelmed with that. They're trying to bring the kids back up because they're far below in reading, and asking, "How do I do that but also bring in global competencies?" As a principal, I need to help teachers see how they can connect the two. They're not separate entities. They need to work in unison with one another.

A high school principal from the Midwest concurred, saying, "Not everyone feels that global learning is as important as I feel it is. Some people want to focus on standards and assessment. We want to link the two together as a way of thinking. Some people feel like it's one more thing on their plate. We try to link it back to it *is* the plate."

Integrating global content and perspectives into tested subject areas helps enrich learning with relevant, real-world examples, therefore serving as a powerful mechanism for engaging all students as they work toward traditional content-area mastery (Lindsay, 2016). I have yet to speak with a school administrator or teacher who hasn't raved about students' enthusiasm toward global learning activities. A suburban middle school principal shared, "Since introducing global competence into the curriculum, we have fewer discipline issues because I think kids are more engaged and more excited about the learning opportunities that they're being given." A rural elementary school principal likewise shared, "Students do get excited. When you can bring in more of a technology base and discuss something with a teacher from somewhere else, the engagement level rises. And typically, when the engagement or excitement level rises, students are more focused and usually get more out of it. I've seen that through several of the lesson plans I've observed that have integrated global tie-ins."

By infusing tested content-area instruction with a real-world context that resonates with students' lives, interests, experiences, and future goals, students see value in what they are learning and are more likely to engage with the standard course of study. As a principal aptly put it, "Moving beyond shallow instruction is more interesting than telling students, 'Read Chapter 1.'" And student engagement, in turn, is correlated with higher grades, test scores, and graduation rates (Klem & Connell, 2004).

School Competition

School choice has been another major policy trend shaping education over the past few decades. Charter schools have come in vogue as innovative alternatives to "failing" public schools, as have voucher programs that provide students with public funding to attend private schools. This can add additional pressure on leaders to emphasize test scores and not lose students—and per-pupil expenditures—to other schools.

This can also create an atmosphere that encourages school leaders to innovate. Adopting global initiatives can entice parents to keep their children enrolled, particularly when you make the link between global initiatives and improving students' academic and cognitive skills. For example, one small, low-income school district in the Southeast adopted global education as a districtwide initiative in part to stop the flow of students to a new charter school. An elementary school principal in that district observed,

> We needed parents to see that there were options available to them in our district and that we were trying to broaden our horizons as a school district to reach the needs of a very diverse population. This let us say, 'We are trying to prepare students for a more globally competitive market. They can be exposed to things that they are not necessarily being exposed to in other school districts and charter schools that surround us.'

An assistant principal in a suburban, more affluent district in the same southeastern state in one of the top-performing schools felt the same competitive pressure from neighboring magnet, charter, and private schools. He brought global education to his school for the same reasons: to prevent losing students to other schools by providing them with a relevant, engaging curriculum that answers the question of why school should matter.

Student Diversity

As populations around the world become more mobile, classrooms are becoming more diverse. In the United States, one in four children under the age of 18 is a first- or second-generation immigrant, and more than 350 languages are spoken in homes across the country (Child Trends, 2018). The population of children under the age of 5 is primarily minority, signaling that the future population of school students will remain diverse. In addition, many regions and towns are experiencing demographic shifts for the first time, leaving schools grappling with how to teach new communities of nonnative English speakers without adequate resources and training. An educator, parent, or community leader concerned about the success of immigrant students might innocuously ask, 'Don't schools need to prioritize helping these students acclimate to their new surroundings and learn English so they can successfully navigate our school system?"

Making immigrant students feel welcome goes beyond teaching them English. It is about validating the language and culture they bring with them, as language and culture are deeply entwined with identity. School leaders have a choice to make in the response to demographic shifts. When schools subtract students' identities by expecting assimilation and devaluing their home language and culture, students disengage from classes or outright resist school authority (Gibson, 1998; Valenzuela, 1999). Conversely, students benefit academically, socially, and emotionally when they can incorporate the dominant school culture into their existing cultural repertoire—rather than replace it—and when bridges are built between school and home (Gibson, 1998; Rothstein-Fisch & Trumbull, 2008). Globally competent teaching takes an additive approach to student diversity, incorporating students' home languages and cultures into the existing curriculum and instruction, communication with families, and special services and events. And when students see themselves in the curriculum, they are more likely to engage and achieve (Ladson-Billings, 1995).

Intercultural communication is another vital aspect of global competence that directly benefits a linguistically diverse student body. You and your staff do not have to become fluent in every language your students speak, but by gaining an understanding of second language acquisition; verbal and nonverbal modes of communication; and the intersection of language, communication, identity, and culture, you can begin to empathize with language learners' needs, help them and their families feel welcome in school, and avoid cultural misunderstandings that could have adverse consequences for students' academic engagement and achievement (Tichnor-Wagner et al., 2019).

Globally competent teaching also models for students how to engage civilly with one another even when peers hold different perspectives, beliefs, and values (Tichnor-Wagner et al., 2019). Whether it's hanging multilingual posters in the hallways to show that you respect the language a student speaks at home, validating perspectives that differ from your own, or facilitating respectful discussions around sensitive or controversial issues, all hold the potential to guide students from varied backgrounds—be they religious, racial, ethnic, or political—and learn to respect and work with one another, a skill that is sorely needed in public civil discourse today.

Poverty

Fifteen million school-aged children in the United States live below the poverty line. This number is disproportionately higher for African American, Latinx, and American Indian children (National Center for Children in Poverty, 2018). Students living in poverty are more likely to have had adverse childhood experiences such as inadequate nutrition, abuse, witnessing or experiencing violence, living with someone with substance addiction, or discrimination that adversely affects physical, cognitive, social, and emotional functioning (Child Trends, 2019). Naturally, students bring these stressors to school with them. A staff member might ask, "Shouldn't meeting students' basic physical and mental health needs take precedence over revamping the curriculum to become globally focused?"

Though teaching for global competence might not ameliorate the most pressing issues these students face (e.g., hunger, violence), it can benefit them in the long term by providing opportunities to help break the cycle of poverty. Global learning can open doors for the jobs of both today and the future by teaching students the skills most valued in the global marketplace. Cultural awareness, cross-cultural competency, and linguistic proficiency are essential skills workers need in our globally connected economy (Committee for Economic Development, 2006; Sodexo, 2015). National Center on Education and the Economy president Marc Tucker (2016) argues that in today's economy of automation and outsourcing, the need for schools to teach higher-level cognitive and noncognitive skills—including an understanding of the perspectives of people from other parts of the world—is paramount.

According to the World Economic Forum's Future of Jobs Report (2018), trending skills for current and future employers include, among others, analytical thinking and innovation; active learning and learning strategies; creativity, originality, and initiative; critical thinking and analysis; complex problem solving; emotional intelligence; and reasoning, problem solving, and ideation—all skills that globally competent teaching develops. By not exposing students to global perspectives and experiences, schools may inadvertently perpetuate an opportunity gap that denies students from low-income backgrounds essential skills to gain employment in a global, knowledge-based economy.

The opportunity for students to see the world beyond their neighborhood can expand their own horizons and future economic prospects, particularly for those in communities hit hard by economic stagnation. As jobs increasingly require cross-cultural understanding and collaboration, intercultural communication, and critical thinking, it is a disservice to deny students opportunities to develop these highly marketable skills just because of their ZIP code, test score, or label. The following observation from a middle school principal is testament to the power of global education to combat inequitable economic opportunities that students in low-income communities face:

> Particularly in areas like here, our students usually come from lower socioeconomic backgrounds. We have students here that will most likely never travel outside of their county. For someone to be a globally competitive student when they get to high school and go to college, they need to know the world outside of the U.S. Global education is a way to give kids opportunity, to show them what they didn't know or may not have seen before and give them the opportunity to make a decision based on that of where they want to go. It's opening their eyes, giving them experiences, and letting them know what's out there beyond their town, their county, or their state. Our students are the students who need that and can really grow and do better for themselves.

Unfortunately, global education has historically been viewed as an "extra" or something confined to elite, wealthy schools or small cohorts of high-performing students. Researchers have found that schools labeled as low achieving consider global education to be a "nice-to-have" rather than a "need-to-have" (Frey & Whitehead, 2009; Gaudelli, 2003). I have toured high schools that have opened world government or global studies courses only to students on the Advanced Placement/International Baccalaureate track and elementary schools where students who are meeting benchmarks in tested subject areas are the only ones who participate in global electives. Because there exists a misconception that global competence only matters to the "elite," as a leader, it is paramount to emphasize that global competence matters for *everyone*.

Global competence provides so much more than a meal ticket. It empowers students to lead the changes they want to see in their own communities and to make a glocal difference (Lindsay, 2016). Taking action on issues of local, regional, or global concern that students deem important is one of the four pillars of global competence in the Asia Society and Council of Chief State School Officers framework (Mansilla & Jackson, 2011) and in the OECD Global Competence Framework (2018). For example, the first goal in the UN's Sustainable Development Goals is No Poverty. Globally competent teaching helps students make connections between global statistics (e.g., "783 million people live below the international poverty line" and "one in nine people in the world today is undernourished") and how they manifest in their local communities and personal experiences. More than that, globally competent teaching prompts students to investigate why poverty exists and empowers students as change agents who can take action to address the root causes they identify.

Social-Emotional Needs

Bullying. Anxiety. Family stressors. Natural disasters. School shootings. Neighborhood violence. Hate speech and hate crimes. Deportations. Addiction. These are just some of the conditions and events that seem to be taking place with greater frequency in communities across the country and can instantly disrupt students' lives, well-being, and education. As schools face increasing pressure to proactively address students' psychological well-being, is it insensitive to teach about issues affecting people elsewhere?

Teaching for global competence simultaneously services students' social-emotional needs. These globally competent teaching elements—of empathy and valuing multiple perspectives; experiential understanding of multiple cultures; creating a classroom environment that values diversity and global engagement; facilitating intercultural and international conversations; developing local, national, and international partnerships; and integrating learning experiences that promote explorations of the world—overlap with the Collaborative for Academic, Social, and Emotional Learning's core social-emotional learning competencies, specifically social awareness (perspective taking, empathy, appreciating diversity, respect for others), relationship skills (communication, social engagement, relationship building, teamwork), and responsible decision making (analyzing situations, solving problems, evaluating, ethical responsibility) (CASEL, 2019). To be clear, globally competent teaching is not a replacement for but rather a complement to social-emotional skill interventions, trauma-informed practices, and counseling as it can help students empathize and respectfully interact with peers regardless of background and process and respond to difficult and complex situations.

Actions to Build Glocal Bridges

Draw upon the following globally competent school leadership attributes to build bridges between the immediate needs and experiences of your students, staff, and school community and integrating global competence into the fabric of your school:

- Facilitating a shared mission and vision.
- Supporting curriculum, instruction, and assessment.
- Advocating and engaging the community.
- Striving for equity and inclusivity.

The examples that follow are not meant to be prescriptive but rather to generate ideas that you can adopt to fit the needs and reality of your specific school context.

Shared Mission and Vision

- Examine your existing school mission and vision. Does it emphasize student achievement? Preparing students for college and career? Making students lifelong learners? Whatever your mission and vision entail, ask staff to reflect on how global competence could be a means toward achieving your visionary goals.

- Open the mission-building process by asking, "What does *global* mean to you? What does *global* look like to you in our school?" The resulting definition that your staff ultimately agrees on can encompass what the school is already doing and future endeavors the school hopes to accomplish.

- If you already have global competence embedded into your school mission, inventory the programs and practices you already have in place that could help attain it. You may be surprised at the number of existing programs and practices you haven't explicitly labeled as "global" but seek to develop the same knowledge, skills, and attitudes. Use these as a starting point for building out a global approach. For example, an elementary school principal's focus on global stewardship arose out of service projects and fundraising (for UNICEF and Heifer International) in which the school had a rich history of participating.

- Survey staff members to see who already has global connections and experiences. You may learn that some teachers conduct regular Skype sessions with classrooms in different countries, have lived or taught abroad, go on annual mission trips, or live in a bicultural household. The experience of staff members both in and beyond the classroom can help shape how your school defines *global* so it builds on teachers' existing practices, interests, and expertise.

Curriculum, Instruction, and Assessment

- Provide scaffolds to help staff make connections between global content and their respective content areas. Global thinking routines are one way to prompt students to connect standards and content to their own lives and the wider world and simultaneously nurture global dispositions (Mansilla, 2016). For example, ask teachers to post four simple questions on their whiteboards:

1. How does ____ affect me?
2. How does ____ affect my neighborhood/community?
3. How does ____ affect my country?
4. How does ____ affect the world?

As a warm-up or end-of-lesson reflection, teachers can complete the sentences using any topic they covered in the lesson—be it a history lesson on the signing of the Declaration of Independence or a science lesson on ecosystems. This activity illuminates for students how they— as individuals, in their local communities, and around the world—are interconnected. As a middle school principal in a small town emphasized, "Global education is all about creating a more well-rounded, connected student—someone who understands what's going on not just in this little part of the world but how this part of the world connects to the bigger picture. How does my community affect my state, my nation, and my world?"

- Use service learning to address both students' local concerns and global issues. If your school already has a service learning program in place, encourage staff to help students find the global implications of the issues they are already addressing. If you are just starting to institute service learning in your school, organize a committee with staff, student, and community member representation. This committee can identify issues of local and global importance and help students learn about, create, and act on parameters for projects that draw upon a variety of local, national, and international perspectives (Singmaster, 2012).

Advocacy and Engagement

- Make explicit the connections between global learning and the issues that parents, community members, and district leaders deem urgent— be it social-emotional learning, reading achievement, or working with

English language learners. A middle school principal in a rural, low-performing school district admitted that just because you see a need for global learning, stakeholders might not: "I know global competence is a real need for our students. It is a real need for our community. Sometimes it's the way it is sold that can be the difficult part. Parents, students, and even teachers are not necessarily going to see it as directly tied to what our current problems are, what we are really facing in the schools."

- Illuminate those connections early and often. Every time you introduce a global initiative to someone new, explain your rationale: "This global initiative will help us with [insert the issue that matters to that stakeholder] because _____." For example, an elementary school principal from the rural Southeast explained how teachers were at first skeptical of global education. With many of the schools in their district receiving failing scores on the state report card, they thought they needed to focus on improving test scores. The principal emphasized the importance of connecting the dots between global learning and long-term student achievement:

  > This is why it's been so important from the administrators' standpoint to let teachers know this is what we need to do for our students. Not just the idea that there's a test out there they have to pass, but making them more globally aware is what in the end is going to make them more successful and make them someone who looks better in the college application process, because they have been able to get exposed to these different types of global concepts and have been in schools where this has been a driving force.

- Provide evidence to key stakeholders that shows how global learning is relevant to the community where you teach. Mapping the Nation (www.asiasociety.org/mapping-nation) provides state-by-state data points on how communities around the country are already globally connected. Click on your state to find statistics for the percentage of residents who speak a language other than English at home, the percentage of jobs connected to international trade, and top export markets. Similarly, the U.S. Census Bureau (www.census.gov/quickfacts) gives a town-by-town breakdown of race, percentage of the population that was born in another country, and the percentage of the population that speaks a language other than English at home.

- Ground your arguments for global competence in the needs and desires of the families your school serves. To understand where families are coming from, examine existing parent surveys or conduct a new one. Hold parent roundtables and coffee chats. Conduct home visits. Ask these simple questions: What do you want your children to get out of school? What are the most pertinent issues for you? From these conversations, see if there are ways to connect the dots between families' desires and global learning outcomes. Remember, do not try to fit a square peg in a round hole. If parents are concerned about playground safety, for example, you will need to address that issue separate from global learning initiatives.

Equity and Inclusivity

- Look up the college entry requirements for local four-year colleges and universities. Odds are, they recommend or require at least two years of a foreign language, with the more selective ones recommending more. If you work in a high school, figure out what percentage of students are fulfilling this requirement, and for those students who aren't, what barriers need to be eliminated to make sure they all have access to language learning and are college-ready? If you work at an elementary or middle school, provide early opportunities for students to learn a second (or third!) language to sow the seeds for this important aspect of college readiness.

- Make sure all students' individual identity markers—cultural, linguistic, ethnic, racial, religious, and others—are valued. This is true whether your student population has recently become more diverse or your school has long served students from diverse cultural and linguistic backgrounds. Global competence is more than a broad knowledge of the world; it begins with an understanding of how each person fits into that world. Therefore, provide opportunities for students to gain an understanding and appreciation of their own culture and ethnicity before helping them gain an appreciation of those from different countries and cultures. As principal Simon Rodberg (2016) of DC International School succinctly stated, "Students can't learn if they have to leave themselves behind" (p. 66). Rodberg went on to describe ways he weaves students' cultural backgrounds into the fabric of the school. For example, at the beginning of the school year, he asks students to share the significance of an artifact from home that will be displayed in a schoolwide cross-cultural garden. Don't be shy to do the same for teachers!

- Incorporate the home or heritage languages of your students when determining language courses and programs. Provide opportunities for students to formally study their home language. Ideally, if there is one predominant language spoken by your nonnative English speaking population, offer a dual immersion program in that language, as dual immersion programs cultivate biliterate and culturally competent students and significantly help English language learners become proficient in English (and achieve higher in math and reading) (Collier & Thomas, 2004; Feinauer & Howard, 2014; Steele et al., 2017).

- Celebrate students' transnational experiences as a method to connect your school to the wider world. A principal with students from the Middle East, Western Europe, and East Asia explained how global education complemented the "United Nations" of her school and surrounding community. Another principal teaching in a community that housed a large military base explained, "A lot of our students have actually lived and traveled abroad. They have lots of international experience themselves. They may leave us, go live someplace abroad, and come back. That international presence in part of our community heritage was a great foundation for studying globalization." Illuminating the global nature of your student body illustrates to staff that the world is not something "out there" to study; it is something in which each of our students is deeply embedded.

Reflection and Action

1. What are the most pertinent needs with which your school is dealing? How does global learning align with these needs?

2. Create a visual to illustrate how you and your school staff are globally connected. With a pin, indicate the location of your school on a world map. Then ask, Where are you and your family members from? Where are your students from? Where have you lived, studied, and traveled? Where are other educators and organizations with whom you've collaborated from? Put a pin in each of the locations staff members mention. With a string, connect each location to the pin representing your school. Keep this visual displayed as a reminder of how you are already making global connections and continue to add to it as your global connections grow.

3. Survey your community to find out where local-global connections are taking place. Dive deep into census-style demographics to see what countries are represented in your school and surrounding community. Explore which businesses, both small and large, have international owners or offices around the world. Identify the various cultural institutions that serve community members. With this information, work with a team of staff members to develop a strategy for incorporating these connections into your global action items—be it statistics to help advocate for global education, a partnership to provide students with internships in a transnational company, or resources to incorporate students' culture into school activities.

4. Survey students to find out what issues and topics matter to them in their lives inside and outside school and what their future aspirations are. Use this information to help make the case for and build out global initiatives in your school.

Garnering Political Will

Darkness cannot drive out darkness. Only light can do that. Hate cannot drive out hate. Only love can do that.

Dr. Martin Luther King Jr.

An elementary school principal in the suburban South was excited about the prospect of bringing Spanish dual immersion and Mandarin language programs to his students. He had learned about the cognitive, social-emotional, and economic benefits of multilingualism, and he understood the importance of setting an early foundation for language development. Over the previous five years, his school had also seen a surge of immigrant students from Central America, and based on research that shows how learning in your first language can help you acquire a second language, he believed that dual language programs would particularly benefit that student population. However, when he took his proposal to the school board, a few vocal parents got upset. They petitioned the language programs and sent a complaint to the superintendent on the grounds that the programs weren't rigorous enough, immigrant students needed to learn English because that was the language of the United States, and schools shouldn't be teaching Chinese community values.

The principal could respond in one of two ways. He could take the "safe" route, acquiescing to the complaints of community members to avoid controversy but at the cost of keeping students in the dark. Alternatively, he could choose a courageous route, pushing back on the pushback by teaching the community the value of understanding different languages and perspectives—but potentially risking his reputation and future job prospects in the district.

It is no easy task to navigate the choppy political waters around teaching globalization, countries, cultures, religions, and languages. By *political*, I mean the power dynamics and conflicts in values and beliefs surrounding education practices, policies, and initiatives (Marshall & Gerstl-Pepin, 2005). To get global initiatives off the ground requires an understanding of who holds authority and influence within your school community and what community members' beliefs are regarding globalization and diversity.

The power dynamics surrounding the adoption and implementation of any new education initiative are complex, to say the least. In what researcher Karl E. Weick (1976) dubbed a "loosely coupled" education system of state and federal policymakers, school boards, superintendents, district leaders, school administrators, teachers, and family and community stakeholders, each maintains distinct decision-making jurisdictions and identity while being responsive to one another. For example, a state legislative body has the authority to pass a graduation requirement that mandates all students take a civics class. District administrators can create a scope and sequence for high school civics teachers to follow, which the school board must approve. Teachers determine what instruction looks like, the actual content that will be covered, and the learning activities that students experience.

At the same time, power is not distributed equally among the people occupying each of these levels. Superintendents wield authority over school administrators. School administrators hold power over teachers. White and wealthier parents may feel more comfortable exerting influence over school personnel than parents who identify with historically marginalized groups and lower socioeconomic statuses. School leaders are situated directly in the crosshairs of making sense of state and district policy demands and the needs of staff, students, and community members. Regardless of where you lead from—the principal's office, the classroom, or a school board seat—you must negotiate policies from the top and the needs of staff, students, and community members on the ground to reshape schools into globally oriented spaces for learning.

For innovative reforms such as globally competent teaching and learning to effectively and sustainably take hold in schools, buy-in from three main stakeholder groups is required:

- **Teachers.** They are the gatekeepers of what students actually learn, and they can choose to minimally comply with or outright close their doors on bringing the world into their classrooms if they don't believe in its importance or relevance.
- **Policymakers.** Superintendents, school board officials, state board of education members, and state representatives hold the power of the purse in funding global initiatives and the power of persuasion from their perch of authority.
- **Families and community members.** This group serves as invaluable partners in promoting students' holistic learning, and they also hold the power of the populace in electing—or pushing out—education officials.

It's important to keep in mind that individuals within these three groups may hold different reasons—reasons that reflect personal values and beliefs—for supporting or pushing against global learning initiatives.

Global is inherently a value-laden word. Some associate it with positive cosmopolitan ideals of progress and diversity. Others cringe as they equate the word with economic insecurity, a lack of agency over local affairs, self-interested elites, and a new social order in which their needs and identities are neglected or devalued. As a leader, being cognizant of and attuned to the value that different stakeholders place on this word is key to building will and excitement across the school community and preventing differences in understanding from spiraling into a public relations crisis.

Barrier: How Do I Overcome Political Pushback to Global Teaching and Learning in My Community?

Whether you are a principal adopting a schoolwide global focus or a teacher leader implementing a unit on climate change or immigration, be prepared for pushback. Pushback can take many forms and come from any number of stakeholders. The following sections highlight the two most common political barriers global education champions have shared with me over the past five years: policy incompatibility and antiglobal attitudes.

(Perceived) Policy Incompatibility

For school leaders, there are many pulls. As outlined in the previous chapter, they range from high-stakes accountability student achievement tests, mandated curriculum, student trauma and mental health issues, and a revolving door of state and federal policies. Initiative fatigue can make educators wary of any new reform as "just one more thing" or "the flavor of the week" soon to be replaced by something shinier.

The truth is that some of these policies do, in fact, directly conflict with global education aims and goals. The public education system in the United States has for centuries promoted a singular national identity that fails to account for the multifaceted cultural, regional, and transnational identities that students simultaneously hold (Banks, 2008; Gaudelli, 2009). Such a curriculum seeks to assimilate rather than validate diverse, global perspectives.

As one example of this, schools in California, Arizona, and Massachusetts for many years mandated English-only instruction (though at the time of this writing, those policies have been reversed). In most states, high-stakes tests are only offered in English. This may cause nonnative English speakers to want their children to be in English-only classrooms out of fear they won't develop the language skills they need to succeed in the U.S. schooling system and cause educators to question the value of teaching students in a different language if they must pass tests in English to access advanced coursework.

In addition, passive forms of policy pushback (i.e., a lack of policy action) can slowly grind globally competent teaching and learning to a halt. Indeed, as school leaders have shared, "It's nobody's emergency" and "There are other fires to put out." If carrots and sticks are tied to state laws focused solely on achievement in reading and math—and not global learning outcomes—then it is logical to focus on the content that is connected to your job security.

Antiglobal Attitudes

Antiglobal sentiments—from policymakers, parents, *and* teachers—can derail efforts to globalize your school. We are living at a time when globalization is both at its peak and receiving intense pushback. Yes, our world is becoming more interconnected through technology, economies, migration, and more. And this comes with great benefits, including increased diversity, enhanced creativity and innovation, access to abundant and affordable high-quality goods and services, and the melding of the world's greatest minds and technologies to solve pressing problems.

The story of a Thai soccer team rescued from the Tham Luang cave in the summer of 2018 provides a perfect example of this last point. Twelve boys and their coach became trapped in an elaborate cave system in a remote town in Thailand after a series of floods. All were eventually rescued by an international team of elite cave divers, experts, and doctors from multiple countries (including Thailand, Australia, China, the United Kingdom, and the United States), who were in turn supported by local villagers who provided meals, massages, and coffee (Mahtani & Wutwanich, 2018).

While this feel-good story of international cooperation dominated international headlines, the dark side of globalism was also rearing its angry head, manifesting itself in the outsourcing of jobs overseas for cheaper labor; the displacement and disappearance of communities, cultures, and environmental ecosystems due to exploitation of land, animals, and people; the legacy of colonialism; and the rise of right-wing identity politics rooted in racism and xenophobia (Andreotti & Pashby, 2013; Banks, 2017; Gaudelli, 2016). Ironically, technology that was created to unite people across borders is often used to barricade people from those whose perspectives and opinions differ. People get their news from outlets that mirror their own values; follow newsfeeds that express their personal political leanings; and are directed to videos, articles, and advertisements based on algorithms that calculate individual preferences.

Due in part to economic and social anxieties brought on by globalization, ethnonationalism is on the rise in the United States and around the world (Potok, 2017). Ethnonationalism is a form of nationalism that defines the nation in terms of a shared ethnic heritage, and it promotes a package of anti-globalization, anti-immigration, and racist beliefs (Manza & Crowley, 2018). Far-right politicians who advocate for closing borders to immigration and commerce and who use hateful, fear-mongering rhetoric have been elected to prominent offices in the United States and Europe. A common thread throughout these successful campaigns has been the practice of exclusionary politics—leaders playing into constituents' fears of unemployment and spinning narratives about immigrants and foreign countries stealing jobs.

Tropes such as "immigrants are taking our jobs" and "our jobs are being outsourced to other countries" instill fear, distrust, and dislike of other countries and cultures. Such rhetoric can also have real consequences. As ethnonationalist narratives enter the mainstream of Western politics, individuals who subscribe to these beliefs come out of the woodwork in greater numbers—casting fear among ethnic minorities who experience increased levels of discrimination, verbal abuse, and violence. In 2016, the Southern Poverty Law Center identified 917 organized hate groups operating in the United States, and a surge in hate crimes was seen in the aftermath of the 2016 U.S. presidential election (Potok, 2017).

Horrific tragedies in Charleston, Charlottesville, and Pittsburgh—at the hands of self-proclaimed white supremacists—have also been seared into the national consciousness. However, hate crimes are nothing new. What we are seeing now is an uptick of a political ideology that has percolated throughout U.S. history—from the genocide of indigenous peoples and the slave trade of the 1600s and 1700s to the rise of the Ku Klux Klan and immigration policies that largely barred those who were not from northern Europe in the early 20th century.

Schools are not detached from the political fray. Instead, it can be quite the opposite. All too often, schools are where cultural wars play out, as is evidenced from the controversies surrounding the teaching of evolution and climate change. In today's politically divisive climate, schools are also where biased-fueled hate occurs. A project by *Education Week* and Documenting Hate reported nearly 500 verified incidents of hate crimes and bias in schools from 2015 to 2017, which mostly targeted black, Latinx, Jewish, and Muslim students (Vara-Orta, 2017).

Therefore, when introducing global competence to your school community, be aware that parents, students, and staff may negatively interpret the word *global*. Education leaders who have championed global learning have shared that some of their constituents equate *global* with *un-American* or believe that "the Chinese and Mexicans are taking our jobs." As one leader told me, this mentality "weighs against a lot of enthusiasm for global education." These global education champions have shared stories of vocal opposition to global learning that include community backlash at public hearings, tweets from parents claiming they won't enroll their students in public school, and a mother putting signs along the road saying that dual immersion programs are bad for children. One elementary school principal in a military community in the Southeast found the required Chinese language elective he introduced to be a tough sell, sharing, "We had some pushback because China is still a communist country, which apparently some people had a huge problem with. . . . We had some people go back to the McCarthy era of the Red Scare and being worried about the communists."

While xenophobia is not a historical blip, depending on the community in which you live, politicians and parents alike may be riding this new wave of nationalist fervor, making global competence a harder sell. How do you respond when a parent bombards you with "Why do you teach Chinese? It's a communist country, and communism goes against everything I hold sacred and believe!" What about when a parent tweets that global education is a ploy of the United Nations to take over American schools and our government? Or when you find out that teachers have gotten together to pray that they won't go to hell for teaching about different world religions?

Solution: Show the Light and Show the Love

It is almost cliché to say that we live in a world that is polarized and divisive, a world where it is all too easy to live in echo chambers that reinforce our own ideologies and where it is all too easy to otherize rather than seek common ground. Instead of practicing the politics of exclusion and telling people who already agree with you what they want to hear, we should lead by practicing the politics of education and empathy. This will help generate will among stakeholders who are vital to making global learning a reality.

Show the Light

Educate potential and active opponents to "global" initiatives about why global competence matters for students. According to one elementary school principal who sent teachers on an annual professional development exchange to Belize,

> There have been pockets of resistance throughout the district. People have asked, "How are you paying for teachers? Why are teachers going to Belize? Are they going on vacation?" This is because people don't truly understand it. We've just taken those comments and turned them into opportunities to educate them about why it's money better spent to spend a week teaching in Belize than it is to stay at the Embassy Suites in Charlotte. I've used misconceptions and snide remarks as opportunities for education.

You can illuminate the value of global learning in the following ways.

Load up on data. Collect and showcase quantitative and qualitative data that make the case for global learning. If you are beginning a partnership with an external organization to help your staff integrate global learning, share reports the organization has generated on the impact of their program. (These are often posted on organizations' websites.) If you are already piloting these programs or practices at your school, share data on how they are affecting student outcomes. Find quick, easy ways to document outcomes that stakeholders in your community care about, such as student engagement, discipline, or attendance. (If you aren't seeing the outcomes you expect, the data should help you reflect on ways you can improve!)

Research has shown positive outcomes for various initiatives that promote global competence development, including project-based learning, language programs, and cultural exchanges—and you can share the results with key stakeholders. For example, project-based learning has been associated with increases in student engagement, language growth, content knowledge, and academic achievement (Duke & Halvorsen, 2017; Holm, 2011; Kokotsaki, Menzies, & Wiggins, 2016). When it comes to language learning, bilingualism is associated with enhanced cognitive development and academic achievement. Dual immersion programs specifically have helped raise test scores on English language proficiency for English language learners and math and reading achievement for both native- and nonnative-speaking students (Collier & Thomas, 2004; Steele et al., 2017). In addition, study abroad for high school students has been linked to an increased motivation for learning; a desire to study, work, or live abroad in the future; and an ability to build relationships with peers from different backgrounds (Engel, 2018).

Quantifying global competence isn't easy. Luckily, qualitative accounts can be just as powerful as numbers—if not more so. They also can provide a more accurate picture of how schoolwide initiatives are affecting students. When I have asked principals to share specific student outcomes they've seen, they share things such as:

- Students relate to challenging issues and extend conversations beyond the classroom.
- Student engagement increases.
- Students believe they have a voice that matters.
- An increase in positive behavior.

- Students become intellectually curious and more willing to take academic risks.
- Students express a desire to explore new places, study abroad, and major in international fields when they go to college.
- Students demonstrate that they care for one another.
- Students enjoy coming to school.

A high school principal in a midwestern college town summarized, "There's no way to quantify that this is what our school is about. It's more than a feeling of test scores and attendance, though it is also true that those have been on the rise the past few years, too. The atmosphere has become more harmonious."

To make global competence more compelling to all stakeholders, collect testimonials from students and staff. For example, a middle school assistant principal made a video in which he interviewed students about the importance of global education and what it means to them. This had a powerful effect on both staff and parents. A K–12 school administrator in Los Angeles used a staff retreat at the beginning of the school year to rally his school around global learning through live student, parent, and teacher testimonials. He explained, "That energizes people and lets them see what's going on. This gets other teachers to think, 'This is amazing. If they did it, then I better get with the program.'"

Have stakeholders experience global learning. Don't just tell stakeholders about the effect of global learning; show them! There is no better way than showing off the important work you, your staff, and your students are doing than by actively involving people in that work. To this end, some schools and districts host events (e.g., parent nights, fairs) with the explicit intention of getting community members to see what a globally focused education entails. These can be fun events that build excitement about global learning or culminating events that give students an opportunity to share their work with an authentic audience.

One elementary school principal whose teachers were just beginning to integrate global competence into their lesson plans held a Global Passport Night at the start of the school year. This event kicked off the school's global focus for parents and students. Each grade level was assigned a country, and each classroom had culturally relevant activities for students and parents. Attendees carried "passports" that got stamped when they visited each "country." Because the school was in an insulated rural community, this activity helped introduce students and their families to the world and built excitement around global integration in the content areas.

For teachers who roll their eyes at the prospect of having "one more thing" to do, show them that global teaching and learning is 1) not one more thing, 2) engaging for students, and 3) fun for teachers! Schedule time for teachers to observe other classrooms in which global competence is already being integrated. You can do this in classrooms in your own school, or you can take a professional learning field trip to a different school with a similar student population. If your schedule doesn't allow for observations, share classroom videos of globally competent teaching and learning in action so teachers see how engaging it can be.

An assistant principal at an elementary school in a rural town shared, "It's that excitement you can bring to the classroom that engages students. We have so many other things that bog us down, the assessments after assessments, the decisions that the legislation makes for us. But the passion, the real reason we got into it was the kids. And when you see what integrating global does with engaging those kids and allowing them to retain knowledge because they've made a deeper connection, it's just amazing."

Time it right. Numerous school and district administrators I've interviewed over the years shared that they had spoken with, surveyed, and promoted global initiatives to parents *before* implementing them. Frontloading the information and ensuring that staff, families, and community members know what you're doing, why you're doing it, and how it will help students will give them the opportunity to ask questions and express concerns.

This allows them to have a voice in the matter, and it gives you a chance to respond with data that can offset misconceptions.

A superintendent of a rural school district spent an entire year educating the school community about the district's new global focus and why it was important for their students. He held 35 community meetings over the course of six months and took almost 20 bus tours with parents, teachers, board members, and administrators to visit a neighboring school district that had already implemented global initiatives. He shared, "When we went to these schools, our stakeholders were astonished with what they saw. Kids were on task and excited about learning, the schools were high energy, and 6-year-olds were speaking two languages. The program really sells itself when you can see it live." Taking the time to build will help facilitate the process of getting the entire community on board.

Show the Love

Educating stakeholders about the value of global competence need not be—and should not be—didactic. It's important to build two-way communication channels to show you care. True caring occurs when the needs of the cared-for are listened to and addressed (Noddings, 1984). Therefore, communication should focus on listening to people who may be dissatisfied with or concerned about global education and determining how to effectively respond to those concerns. The active listening skills we teach students as they engage in intercultural conversations apply equally to adults. Active listening involves asking thoughtful questions based on what you hear, confirming and clarifying what you heard before sharing your response, and recognizing perspectives with which you might not agree. When someone is talking, you shouldn't be silently planning your response or interrupting them. Instead, you should be immersed in what that person is saying.

Engage in ongoing dialogue. Nancy Gibbs, former editor-in-chief for TIME, wrote, "Just giving people more information, whether about climate change or crime rates or vaccines, does not pave a road to common ground" (2018, para. 8). Telling stakeholders that global competence is important—even providing the data to go with it—may not be enough to convince them to support this work. However, engaging in an ongoing conversation that gives stakeholders an opportunity to share their understandings and beliefs about global learning may be a step toward changing negative perceptions. Create an open dialogue with community members to address concerns; don't wait until a parent complains about a project his or her child is doing on world religions or a petition starts circulating about ending the Chinese immersion program. Begin dialogues about global teaching and learning early and engage in them often.

Provide multiple access points for parents and community members. Community meetings create a space for these initial conversations to occur, and it's a good idea to structure those meetings so you succinctly explain the what, how, and why of your global learning objectives and leave plenty of time for questions and answers. As an administrator in a rural district shared, "Community meetings definitely gave us a step up because people were involved. They had the opportunity to ask questions and have their concerns validated or squelched. They felt like they knew what was going to take place. I think it was because of that very thoughtful planning of implementation that we encountered little resistance." Hold meetings several times in different locations during the year. Keep in mind that some places, such as community centers, might make it easier for parents to attend. For those who cannot attend, record the meetings and post the videos online so families can watch at their convenience. (One principal shared with me how she intentionally presented at school board meetings because she knew those meetings were recorded and broadcast on TV for families to see.) This will help spread the information and allow those who can't attend the meetings in person to still benefit from them.

Opening your door for one-on-one conversations is another way to get on the same page as parents and staff members who may be reticent to global efforts. An urban elementary school principal shared how she had one-on-one conversations with teachers who made comments such as "It's really hard for me to integrate these types of ideas into my classroom" and "I don't see the need." She would meet these teachers in their classrooms and work with them to figure out different ways global themes could be incorporated into the curriculum they were already responsible for covering.

Likewise, try to use as many asynchronous methods of communication as possible. This could include newsletters, emails, or videos and presentations on your school's website or social media accounts. A middle school assistant principal, for example, created a digital global education newsletter for the community, used Twitter and Facebook to promote the themes and concepts students were studying, and shared a YouTube video that showcased students' work and ideas about why global education was important to them. The great thing about these types of digital platforms is that they also allow more— and possibly more convenient—opportunities for parents to respond (e.g., through direct messages and comments).

If you are a school administrator, make sure you communicate with teachers about how you will support them as they teach about global issues that some parents may consider controversial (e.g., immigration, climate change, religion). This could entail, for example, instructing teachers to send parent complaints directly to your office or sending letters home in advance to show your support for a potentially controversial unit so parents don't feel blindsided when their children come home discussing an issue from a perspective they might not agree with.

Meet stakeholders where they are. Be mindful that the language you use doesn't alienate stakeholders. If *globalism* is a hot-button issue in your town, avoid that specific word. As a suburban middle school administrator in the Southeast explained, "Global themes that our school addresses include sustainability and recycling. We don't mention global warming because parents don't want the school teaching it because they think it's a pseudoscience. However, this is part of the curriculum and is covered on state end-of-year tests. As long as you don't say *global warming*, it's fine."

Some public pushback has come from stakeholders' misunderstandings of global education as indoctrinating students to become citizens of a global world order. Recognize this misconception by explaining how learning about the world does not replace learning about our country and the diverse cultures within it. An elementary school principal in a military town emphasized, "We reinforce the fact that we are American and we're proud of that every day. But that doesn't mean we don't respect other cultures and try to understand them." She reinforces this notion by having U.S. patriotic symbols throughout the school alongside murals representing all the continents.

Likewise, a suburban middle school assistant principal in the South explicitly tells families at the beginning of the year that global learning is the exact opposite of indoctrination. "It is about exposing students to different perspectives and [allowing them] to form their own opinions based on evidence. My goal is for students to see both sides and then form their own opinions, ideas, and thoughts, whether I agree with them or not." He arrived at this position after feedback from parents revealed their fear that school would flip students on their political parties.

You can meet teachers where they are by recognizing they might view global competence as an additional burden to their schedule. Introduce global competence as something that is layered onto—rather than added to—existing curriculum. As one principal acknowledged, "Anything new has to pass the sniff test of 'Is this relevant for what I do in my classroom?'"

Agree to disagree—up to a point. Show that you are willing to listen to opinions with which you might not agree. Giving people the space to air their concerns builds good will by making them feel valued. It also provides you with a deeper understanding of how to address apprehensions effectively. The Anti-Defamation League (2017a) recommends, "As you engage in conversations with people with whom you differ, it's always a good idea to remember that they come to those positions with their own unique history, background, perspective and experiences and that is ultimately what is driving them" (para. 7).

A district administrator from the South explained how economic globalization caused people in his school community to oppose global learning: "There are still people who see the rest of the world as the People Who Shuttered the Textile Mill. That's who the enemy is. My life is not as good as it used to be and it's somebody else's fault: China, Malaysia, Vietnam, or wherever it was that that textile mill moved." There is truth—and real pain—in the underlying source of this community's apprehension toward global learning. Indeed, multinational corporations that outsource jobs overseas have caused a sharp economic decline in many parts of the United States, from textile mills in North Carolina to steel manufacturing in the Rust Belt. Nevertheless, the conclusion that those parts of the world with cheaper labor are "the enemy" is where you can make headway in changing hearts and minds.

An elementary school principal met with a parent who was opposed to the new Chinese language elective the school had introduced. When he asked the parent what his specific concerns were, the parent responded, "China is a communist country and they steal our jobs." After hearing this, the principal explained that learning Chinese would actually enhance his child's job prospects since China is an important business partner and "we don't want to limit our opportunities for our students." Another principal noted that the argument that "global education will make students more marketable" resonated in his economically stagnant rural community that was largely resistant to change. In that same community, a K–8 principal learned that parents were reluctant to enroll their children in the school's Spanish dual immersion program because they did not know the language and feared they wouldn't be able to help their students complete homework and other class assignments. This led the principal to provide language supports for parents of enrolled students.

Creating a safe space to air opinions is a delicate balance. Although you want to create an atmosphere in which students, parents, and staff feel comfortable expressing themselves, you also have to establish a firm line on the type of speech that should not be tolerated: that which makes students and community members feel unwelcome, unsafe, or both.

The Anti-Defamation League offers strategies for respectful conversations, which include deciding on ground rules that answer the questions "What do we need to feel safe and respected?" and "What does respectful discussion look, sound, and feel like?" Rules might include the following:

- Listen actively.
- Don't attack other people.
- Don't interrupt.
- Don't use biased language.
- Don't call other people names.

People engaged in respectful conversations challenge others when those rules are broken and educate people when they use offensive language they don't know is offensive. (See the Anti-Defamation League's Guidelines for Achieving Bias-Free Communication: www.adl.org/education/resources/tools-and-strategies/guidelines-for-achieving-bias-free-communication.)

In addition to speaking up when you hear stereotypical or biased language, it's important to speak up when you hear "alternative facts" or blatant misinformation. Be prepared to help differentiate between myths and facts about global education, globalization, immigration, and people of various racial, ethnic, religious, and national groups. For example, if a parent says that immigrants don't want to learn English, explain that, according to the U.S. Census, over half of immigrants speak English well or very well (Teaching Tolerance, 2011). If a teacher says she doesn't feel comfortable teaching about Islam because Muslims identify with terrorists, explain that violent extremists are a small minority of those who identify with the Muslim faith, the vast majority of Muslims reject an extremist interpretation of Islam, and terrorist acts around the world have been committed by people who ascribe to a wide range of belief systems (Anti-Defamation League, 2017b). Whether you are presenting at a school board meeting or speaking one-on-one with a parent, don't shy away from correcting offensive language and misinformation whenever you hear it.

Start incrementally. If, through your initial dialogues, you find general apathy or pockets of resistance to teaching global competence, consider starting with a pilot program. A school board member who had supported global education across his district observed, "Once you start forcing things, that's where you get resistance." Making programs voluntary can help convince those on the fence while not ruffling too many feathers. Furthermore, starting with a smaller, more passionate group can generate will as it allows you to provide a proof-point for the benefits of global teaching and learning. For school staff, this might involve focusing global integration efforts on a particular grade level, content-area team, or professional learning community. To assuage parents' concerns, begin by providing voluntary or elective global studies or language classes. Other opt-in programs could include global certificate programs, electives that have a global spin (e.g., environmental science, foods from around the world, international relations), or extracurricular programs (e.g., student clubs, exchange trips, study abroad, afterschool programming).

Slowly building pockets of success can inspire others to infuse global teaching and learning. Share and celebrate the results of your pilot programs. Use data from these pilots and the passion of those who participated in them to build support for policy changes or to boost enrollment in the programs. A high school principal in a Northeast suburb shared how his school first introduced global learning through two optional programs, an environmental club and a global citizenship certificate. Over a decade, the popularity of these two programs grew so much that global citizenship and the environment became obvious core values for the entire school, and students demanded more global activities and electives. He explained, "There's a contagion around it. When a passionate group of people gets organized, they pull in other allies, the momentum builds, and it ripples out." More than halfway down the coast, a former superintendent who brought global competence to her southeastern district had the same experience: "I tell people all the time, if you can build a pocket of success, you can expand a pocket of success, because most people want to be part of something successful."

Remember that a journey of a thousand miles begins with a single step. Sometimes to go big, it's best to start small. Successfully generating will among stakeholders can be a particular challenge as it can be a bit of a chicken-or-the-egg situation. When political will exists for schools to pursue global competence, students will develop a sense of open-mindedness, respect for those from different backgrounds, and a desire to cooperate across cultural, religious, and national borders. Such dispositions can mitigate ethnonationalism, making students and the community more open to global learning. However, if schools do not incorporate global competence in communities where there is pushback, students may not have an opportunity to learn otherwise and resistance will continue. This is why being persistent in generating will is so incredibly important.

Actions to Build Political Bridges

Apply the following globally competent school leadership actions to build politically sound rationales, which can in turn build will among the many school and community stakeholders whose support you will need to jump-start global learning initiatives.

- Facilitate a shared mission and vision.
- Advocate and engage the community.
- Manage operations and resources.
- Strive for equity and inclusivity.

The following are examples to get you started.

Shared Mission and Vision

- As you work on embedding global competence into your school's mission and vision, provide multiple methods for communicating information to staff, parents, and community members. Offer spaces for stakeholder groups to openly and safely articulate ideas, concerns, and questions. Ask questions such as "What does global learning mean to you? What should it look like in our school? What would you want out of it? What value do you see in it?"
- Include parents and community members on global planning teams or task forces; hold quarterly or biannual check-ins with students, staff, and community members; and set aside time for open comments at school meetings. Show that you are listening by being responsive to

concerns and questions. When stakeholders feel like they have a voice in shaping the mission and vision, they will be more likely to want to adhere to it.

- Emphasize a holistic vision of education and deemphasize standardized tests as the be-all-end-all of student learning. One effective way to mitigate pushback is by creating a culture of learning around the broader goal of education: fostering productive workers and thoughtful citizens. By reinforcing this deeper *why* of education, stakeholders are able to see that global competence addresses this goal.

Advocacy and Engagement

- Before beginning any global initiative, take the temperature of your school community. Whether it's starting up a dual immersion program, applying to become an International Baccalaureate World School, or forging a partnership with a school overseas, survey parents and staff on their appetite for it. In the survey, explain what the program is, why you are doing it, and what you hope it will accomplish. Then ask them the following questions:

  1. Is this program something you would want teachers and/or students to participate in? Why or why not?
  2. Is this program something you would want to be involved with?
  3. What questions, comments, or concerns do you have about this program?

  The answers you receive will help you identify supporters and whom you need to convince—and in what ways.

- Build a rationale for global competence that explicitly addresses concerns key stakeholders have raised. Use this rationale consistently when introducing new initiatives. For example, if parents are concerned about their children getting jobs when they graduate, make the case that global competence will make students more marketable. If community members believe that anything global is inherently un-American, point out that military leaders espouse the importance of global competence—particularly speaking multiple languages and understanding different cultures—as vital for national security.

- Devise a communication plan for community outreach for each new global initiative you want to implement. These plans should include *frequent* and *varied* forms of communication (e.g., newsletters, parent nights, town halls, parent and teacher surveys, individual conversations, special events) and allow for two-way dialogues. Be sure to outline whom you will talk to, when you will talk to them, and in what formats.

- Jump on every opportunity to serve on committees, commissions, and panels that advocate for global learning to policymakers. This could be presenting to your school board or sitting on a district or statewide global education task force. Bring anecdotes and hard data to articulate why global competence is important (e.g., demographic and economic shifts in your community) and how students have benefited from global learning experiences.

- Identify a key voice of authority and influence in your community to be a global education champion. For example, call on the business community to explain to policymakers and school boards why global competence matters for the local economy and for students' future job prospects. Ask your superintendent—or someone visible within your district office—to celebrate teachers who have piloted global initiatives. These influential champions can help inspire others to get on board.

Operations and Resource Management

- Strike a balance between putting money where your mouth is and not spending any money. Providing materials, time, and other resources toward global learning is an effective way to show teachers that globally competent teaching is a priority and will therefore increase their likelihood of doing it. Funding tends to be a zero-sum game in education. Therefore, putting too much money and materials into global learning could cause pushback if that money is taken away from other popular programs.

Equity and Inclusivity

- Reflect on biases that influence your own perceptions of different cultures and the ways in which you interact with members of your school community. The Anti-Defamation League (2007) has a helpful self-assessment of anti-bias behavior, which asks questions such as "I look at my own attitudes and behaviors as an adult to determine the ways they may be contributing to or combating prejudice in society," "I avoid stereotyping and generalizing other people based on their group identity," and "I am open to other people's feedback about ways in which my behavior may be culturally insensitive or offensive to others."

- Establish clear schoolwide norms of tolerance and respect so students, families, and staff feel comfortable sharing their personal beliefs and perspectives. Introduce these norms at the beginning of the school year, encourage teachers to model them in their classrooms, and hang posters on walls that reinforce these norms with conversation starters for respectful dialogues. Examples include "I think ____ because ____," "I'm uncomfortable with ____ because ____," and "I hear you saying ____, but I disagree because ____."

- Avoid making assumptions about stakeholders' beliefs and values surrounding global education. Just because a young student immigrated from Mexico doesn't mean that his parents will want to enroll him in a Spanish dual immersion program. Just because a student comes from a different country doesn't automatically mean she has a high level of global competence. As one high school principal of a diverse city in the Midwest explained, "Many people will think that because our kids are from all over, of course they understand the world. But that's not the case. Most students are coming from homogenous cultures, and often with a jaded perspective. It's not unusual for them to have not seen someone of a different race or have had to interact with someone from a different religion. Then they come to our school, and they are placed in a classroom with a lot of heterogeneity. Many who have come from a survival environment haven't had the time or the need to look elsewhere. It's a stretch to have them look at things from a different lens, especially a lens that they think is biased."

Reflection and Action

1. Survey school community stakeholders on their beliefs and interpretations around globalization and diversity. Do any of your data results surprise you? What action steps might you take to educate your community on the importance of global learning for students?

2. Create a list of the key stakeholders you'll need to get on board to make global learning a reality. What teachers, school and district leaders, and community members are key influencers and/or decision makers? What concerns might they have? How might you address those concerns? What evidence and anecdotes could you share with them that will help illuminate the importance of this work?

5

Wrangling Resources

When without resources, depend on resourcefulness.

Sun Tzu

"There's not enough money and too many mandates." This may as well be the mantra for any educator asked to implement a new initiative. Whether implementing new science standards, a new reading curriculum, a new way of designing lessons, or a new instructional approach to teaching English language learners, all educators will tell you they need more time. More time for learning about the initiative, more time for planning, and more time for getting comfortable with implementation. When school leaders are faced with new policy directives, they'll likely say they need a bigger budget. A budget for instructional materials, new staff to provide implementation support, and substitute teachers so staff can attend professional development.

It's no surprise that time and money are not on the side of schools. The demands, pushes, and pulls piled onto educators are constantly accumulating. *Unfunded mandate* is a painfully common term in the education lexicon, and it is often accompanied by the argument that if a mandate isn't funded, then schools aren't going to do it. Unfortunately, "unfunded" is the current state of global education. Even for states that have passed global education policies, those policies often have no purse-strings attached.

Yes, time and money are perennial challenges, but they are not insurmountable obstacles. The resourceful leader will find that existing policies, programs, practices, and budgets can be fertile soil for growing global learners. Viewing global competence as something to be integrated into existing content areas and professional learning can augment learning without overcrowding teachers' plates or depleting already skeletal budgets.

Barrier: Where Do I Find the Time and Funding to Start Global Initiatives?

While teachers' to-do lists always seem to be growing longer, the day is not. Just as sure as there are 24 hours in every day, when asked to implement yet another new initiative, teachers will commonly—and understandably—respond, "Where am I supposed to fit this in?"

With mountains of mandates to climb over—and between state testing, teacher evaluations, and paperwork for referral and intervention programs—it may seem impossible to find the time for teaching global competence. The American Federation of Teachers and the Badass Teachers Association (2017) found that teachers averaged over 50 hours of work per week and reported working more than their regularly scheduled hours up to 13 or 14 days per month. With this in mind, it may seem like the only place for global education is the backseat.

Furthermore, even if you believe wholeheartedly that global competence is a vital learning outcome, it is not the only thing you will want to tackle in a given school year. You may have students who are grade levels behind in reading and math, school safety concerns, students coping in the aftermath of a traumatic event, or a new coaching structure for professional learning that needs to be introduced. These may understandably seem more urgent. After all, don't students need foundational literacy and math skills? Doesn't your school need to focus on increasing performance on the high-stakes tests? As one elementary school principal observed,

Because teachers are judged off of testing and are under a lot of stress to perform, they feel like their hands are tied a bit, and a new initiative like global awareness is taking them away from what they need to be focusing on. The tested grades are even more hesitant to go along with the global lessons because they know they have a test coming so have to push, push, push to cover all of the materials.

On top of that, very few school, district, or state budgets have any kind of funding earmarked for global learning. Most schools have felt the economic pinch after the Great Recession of 2008 with a sharp decline in state and local funding. These effects are still being felt a decade later. Twenty-nine states still provide less overall school funding per student than they did in 2008 (Leachman, Masterson, & Figueroa, 2017). Even before the economic downturn, multiple studies reported insufficient and inconsistent state and government funding for global education (Cruz & Bermudez, 2009; Frey & Whitehead, 2009; Wiley, 2001). Teachers already spend their own money on classroom supplies. By one account, 94 percent of teachers spent their own money during the 2014–2015 school year on classroom supplies without reimbursement, spending an average of $479 (National Center for Education Statistics, 2015–2016). As one principal remarked, "I can see where global education would be pushed into that pile of 'this is just one more thing the state is asking us to do that they're not financially supporting.'"

Perhaps to no one's surprise, 50 percent of teachers who responded to a 2016 survey of ASCD *SmartBrief* readers did not incorporate global competence into their teaching either because they felt as though they did not have the time or because it wasn't in their curriculum (ASCD, 2016). As one respondent summarized, "We are mandated to teach a specific curriculum and there's no room for deviation. There's not time to fit anything outside the curriculum in, and finding resources is time consuming." How do you respond to barriers that are seemingly out of your locus of control?

Solution: Weave Global Initiatives into What You Are Already Doing

Unfortunately, you can't slow down the speed of Earth's daily rotation to sneak an extra hour or two into the day. You might not have the power to increase the number of professional development hours per school year or change the scope and sequence that teachers must cover in the curriculum. You can, however, make choices based on the resources you have that reflect a firm commitment to global learning and that will help develop globally competent teachers and learners. You can also be resourceful with the time at your disposal by teachers' existing professional development and infusing global learning into the content teachers are responsible for teaching.

Integrate Global Content and Resources into Existing Standards, Curricula, and Schoolwide Initiatives

Global competence is best taught within and across disciplinary studies—not as its own separate subject area. Encouraging teachers to integrate global learning into classroom instruction kills two birds with one stone: it helps solve the issue of time and teaches global dispositions, knowledge, and skills in the most effective way (Mansilla & Jackson, 2011; Tichnor-Wagner, Parkhouse, Glazier, & Cain, 2016). As the OECD and Asia Society (2018) argued, "Disciplinary knowledge and skills are not simply what one learns in school with little purpose beyond that. Instead, they are tools for interpreting the world; explaining phenomenon; solving problems; asking informed questions that get at fundamental truths that may not be obvious; and making the world a better, more peaceful, more productive, and more equal place" (p. 20).

Globally competent teaching is a lens through which we can view *all* teaching and learning within and across content areas. Remind teachers that globally competent teaching is not another slice of pie on their plate; rather, it is the whipped cream, chocolate drizzle, and strawberries that make the pie enticing, rich, and delicious. Of course, putting on a global lens can be overwhelming when teachers feel like they need to focus their time elsewhere. As one elementary school principal shared,

One of the hardest things, and I think this is a challenge when introducing anything new, is to help teachers see that this isn't something else they have to do and how to connect what they're already doing with building global competence within students. That mindset piece was one of the biggest challenges initially, especially working in a school where students are underperforming and coming from homes where they have a lot of needs. The teachers are overwhelmed with that and trying to bring the kids back up because they're far below in reading. Of course they are going to ask, 'How do I do that but also bring in these global competencies?'

How, then, can a leader institute global integration as a norm for schoolwide instruction without seeming to take time away from other important needs or add something else to an already overcrowded schedule? The key is helping teachers understand that global competence and academic development are intimately connected.

First, help all school staff recognize that global competence is, as one principal explained to me, "a mindset more than a discipline. It's a way of going about doing what you're already doing." A global mindset allows you to look at whatever it is you are teaching—the plot of a story in elementary school, exponents in middle school math, persuasive writing in high school language arts—and make connections to a global issue or see that content from various viewpoints (Tichnor-Wagner et al., 2019).

Prod teachers to identify areas where global content and perspectives fit naturally into their scope and sequence. For example, when teaching earth science, you can compare and contrast ecosystems in different parts of the world or investigate the effect of climate change on various ecosystems. In language arts, you can incorporate books and stories from a diverse array of authors that take place in settings around the world. Global perspectives even have an important place in the most nationalist oriented subject area: U.S. history. When teaching about the American Revolution, ask students to explore the perspectives and experiences of American colonists, enslaved people, British officials, and indigenous communities. Even mathematics, the so-called universal language, isn't very universal at all. Different parts of the world tackle operations such as multiplication and division in a variety of ways and annotate decimal points using different punctuation marks. There are also endless options for applying math skills to solve real-world problems. (See www.globalmathstories.com for inspiration!)

As described in Chapter 2, this infusion of global issues and perspectives enhances what teachers are already teaching without taking time away from the curriculum they have to cover, and it is done in a way that provides real-world relevance and engagement for students. As a middle school principal put it, "We're not about creating whole new lessons; we are 'plussing' the lessons you've done." Once you've handed out metaphorical global glasses to your staff, provide them with tools to document their work. And, rather than add additional paperwork, "plus" the tools your school already uses. For example, add a global connections section to your lesson plan templates or observation protocols, and explicitly show where global integration aligns with state- or district-mandated evaluation rubrics.

In addition to content-area integration, weave global learning into existing schoolwide initiatives. For example, an elementary principal augmented the school's prior focus on Stephen Covey's seven habits for leadership to create a global leadership theme. A middle school principal piggybacked global learning onto a new schoolwide technology push, emphasizing to staff that students could use devices to conduct research on global topics and connect with other classrooms through virtual exchanges. Blending initiatives together in a way that allows staff to see how current practices and new initiatives work together can lead to deeper implementation and sustainability (Coburn, 2003), and it can simultaneously consolidate precious resources.

Carve Out Time

It's true that an effective integration of global learning can help alleviate overcrowded plates. However, the reality is that you still must carve out some time to teach your staff how to do it. And because time is a finite resource, finding that time is a process of give and take. If teachers are going to dive deep into a global issue, you have to allow them to sometimes miss other units they would have otherwise taught. Giving this discretion also must come with the acknowledgment that they might not be able to cover every mandated standard and that as their designated evaluator, you are fine with that. As one principal shared, the greatest payoff came when he accepted that and gave "permission for teachers to make room for going deep into certain areas related to global competence by carefully thinking through what other things could be left out."

It is equally important to give teachers time and space during existing professional development days to understand key concepts related to global competence and how to incorporate it into their pedagogy. "Global integration is a work in progress. It doesn't come naturally to everybody," one principal admitted. Therefore, it's not enough just to allow teachers to integrate global competence into existing courses and curriculum. You must also account for the time it will take to train teachers to incorporate global thinking and to plan out thoughtful lessons and units. This is critical. School leaders who are committed to global competence must build time into the schedule for professional learning and lesson planning.

The amount of time you carve out ultimately depends on where your school is starting from and the steps you want to take. Inserting global content into more traditional lesson plans will look different from walking staff through the steps of integrating global issues into project-based learning frameworks, especially if teachers have yet to dive into the ins and outs of project-based learning pedagogy. As an elementary school principal in a Midwest town explained, "It takes a lot of time and energy for teachers to develop a project-based learning unit that they can implement in their class on Monday."

There are various places on the school calendar where you can schedule global professional learning. In lieu of other professional development activities, you can have teachers complete quarterly online modules that walk them through the process of writing and implementing lessons that integrate global issues. You can hold faculty meetings devoted to sharing best practices around global integration. You can use professional development days over the summer to give teachers time to delve into how they will integrate global learning in the content areas. (See Chapter 6 for an in-depth discussion on staff capacity building.) These examples highlight the importance of creating dedicated time to address global competence development and the multiple pathways through which it can be achieved.

So where do you find that time? This is where, as a leader, you must make a choice to prioritize global learning over other initiatives during existing professional development slated on the calendar. If your school already has weekly professional learning communities (PLCs), encourage the formation of a global competence cohort or request that staff use part of that time to plan lessons with a global focus. As one middle school teacher explained, "Taking time in PLCs has made it more manageable for the teachers to do, because it's what they do anyways." If your school requires professional development over the summer, set aside some of that time to introduce strategies for integrating global topics and perspectives. If your school has monthly staff meetings, devote 10 minutes to let teachers share best practices for global integration, which can be especially powerful for cross-pollinating ideas across grade levels and departments.

As with classroom teaching, fitting global competence into existing professional development might mean that something else has to be taken away. A K–8 principal of a global-themed school in a low-performing district shared, "The best thing our district did to support us was to take a bunch of other things off of our plates. So instead of having eight million initiatives going on at any given time, our district has done well to say global education is going to be our focus."

Work with Existing Budgets

Global learning doesn't necessarily demand a huge financial investment. For teachers to connect everyday lessons to global contexts, schools don't need to hire an entire new department or overhaul the existing curriculum.

Existing funds and resources already at your disposal can augment global learning. Therefore, the resourceful leader starts by taking stock of what's already available. Inventory your school's instructional tools, materials, and programs to see what aligns with your vision (Reimers, 2017). What technology does your school have that would allow students to connect with peers in different parts of the world? What literature and reading materials do you have in the school library that represent perspectives from diverse countries and cultures? What languages does your school already teach? Which electives and student clubs are already established at your school?

Don't forget to examine the capacity, wisdom, and passion of your staff. Rather than hire new positions, reallocate responsibilities. Among your administrative team, identify a global coordinator who will serve as the go-to person for questions staff have about integrating global content, function as the lead contact for external partnerships and exchanges, share global resources with staff, and help coordinate professional learning. If you already have instructional coaches, train them as global integration coaches. See if anyone on staff has interest in volunteering to lead specific global programs or events. For example, in an IB World School I visited, a 4th grade teacher passionate about global learning volunteered to become the liaison for the sister school partnership they had with a school in Mexico. In a small rural high school, a social studies teacher organized the school's first Global Fest, where students presented projects that proposed solutions to global problems.

If a new teaching position *does* open up at your school, use it as an opportunity to fill a gap in your global or world language course catalogue (e.g., hiring a Mandarin language teacher) or to hire a content-area or grade-level teacher who can demonstrate a commitment to globally competent teaching. Things you might look for in a candidate include experience living, working, or teaching in different countries or with people from different cultural backgrounds; coursework or training on globally competent teaching practices; and specific ideas they have about how to integrate global competence into instruction.

Finally, determine how state and federal funding streams you have at your disposal can be reallocated for global learning. For example, Federal Title II funding under the Every Student Succeeds Act supports professional development for educators that is sustained, collaborative, job embedded, data driven, classroom focused, and teacher led (U.S. Department of Education, 2016). You can use these funds to build the infrastructure for collaborative global unit planning or to reimburse attendance at global education workshops. A principal who received a federal magnet grant used that money to become a global studies dual immersion magnet school and was able to hire instructional coaches for that purpose. Remember, due to the fickle nature of politics, funding that is available one year may disappear the next, or new budget lines may suddenly appear. Therefore, when new state and federal education budgets are approved each year, it is a helpful exercise to examine the categories of funds and how they might align with global learning efforts.

Everything has a price tag. If you use Title II funds to bring in outside facilitators, that comes at the cost of using those funds for, say, literacy coaches. In interviews with school leaders, language learning has commonly emerged as being particularly difficult to fund. The biggest costs are associated with hiring qualified language teachers and purchasing new instructional materials for dual immersion classrooms. However, as a school leader from a charter school in urban California emphasized, it's a matter of choice to allocate money in the budget and then to protect that budget. "It's about making strategic choices with what you have. For example, you make the choice to forgo building a virtual reality lab versus paying for subs to get teacher planning time. You can get as much equipment as you want, but if you aren't preparing educators to effectively use it, then it doesn't matter."

Just because your district or state doesn't have a global education budget line doesn't mean you should abandon the search for funds. Be entrepreneurial. Seek out grants from philanthropies and foundations. Form partnerships with local businesses and organizations. Once you start sleuthing around, you might be surprised by the number of local businesses, community-based organizations, and foundations that are looking to contribute to innovative or successful education causes. Parents and community members can also provide "in-kind" support as guest speakers who make connections between their personal and professional experiences and the wider world. For example, a high school principal from Massachusetts, determined to fund a Japanese exchange, personally called local businesses to sponsor the program. Through his efforts, the program received sponsorship from a booster's club, a car dealership, a water company, a local bank, a celebrity-chef restaurant, and the local little league. The Boston Red Sox even gave the students a free tour of Fenway Park and the Boston Celtics provided tickets to the exchange students and their host families. It never hurts to reach out; the worst thing that can happen is that an organization says no.

There's also a handful of national organizations that fund this work. DonorsChoose is a source to ask for global resources both large and small—from world maps for every classroom to class sets of multicultural books. The Longview Foundation awards small grants for innovations in international education, with a particular focus on promoting integration of international content into state standards, out-of-school programming, career and technical education, literacy, and U.S. history. Empatico is an organization that provides tools for educators of students age 6–11 to connect with classrooms across the United States and around the world. They also provide Spark Empathy Grants of up to $5,000 to help implement virtual exchange programs in schools. For older students, the Stevens Initiative funds grants to educational institutions and nonprofits to run virtual exchange programs between youth in the United States and the Middle East and North Africa that promote global competence. The Fulbright Teachers for Global Classrooms Program is sponsored by the U.S. Department of State and offers grants to alumni to continue their global learning and implement global projects at their school and beyond.

Finally, don't hesitate to roll up your sleeves and engage your school community in some good old-fashioned fundraising to pay for global programs. To help students pay for a Spanish immersion trip to Costa Rica, one principal shared, "We've had a lot of bake sales. We've also collected cans, held yard sales, and had car washes, all of whose proceeds went into the Costa Rica account to help low-income families cover the cost." Through a lot of sweat equity on everyone's part to make it happen and by allowing families to pay the costs in installments over the course of a year or two, all students' trip costs were paid off. Other school and district leaders have started foundations and scholarships to pay for short-term study abroad programs. As many leaders have acknowledged, these trips are expensive, but it is inequitable not to give students such lifechanging opportunities.

In sum, prioritize, prioritize, prioritize. Yes, there are a million things that schools are expected to do to promote student success. However, putting global learning at the top of that list opens up incredible possibilities and numerous resources your school can access to make implementation successful.

Actions to Build Integrative Bridges

Apply the following global competence leadership skills to effectively reallocate and accrue resources to support global learning:

- Support curriculum, instruction, and assessment.
- Establish a collaborative professional community.
- Manage operations and resources.

The examples that follow can serve as a starting point.

Curriculum, Instruction, and Assessment

- Provide paid time over the summer or during professional development days during the school year for teachers to review their grade-level and/or subject-area curriculum map and determine areas where they can "layer" global themes and concepts onto existing standards and required learning outcomes. These planning sessions should focus on two key questions: What type of connections to global issues and perspectives can I make to this standard? What teaching materials can I use to provide students with multiple global perspectives? If your school is new to this work, start by having teachers identify one unit in one subject area.

- Add a global learning component to the lesson plan templates that teachers in your school already use. This could take the form of a global learning objective that aligns to a specific global competence attribute (e.g., recognizing different perspectives) or an element of globally competent teaching (e.g., facilitating international and intercultural conversations).

- The world is a vast place, which may overwhelm teachers as they seek to figure out where and when they can include all the places, people, topics, and issues they want to tackle. To ameliorate this, provide manageable entry points. Work with your staff to institute monthly global themes (e.g., aligned to the UN Sustainable Development Goals) that teachers can integrate into their instruction. Alternatively, ask teachers to select a country, region, or continent to focus on throughout the year.

- Examine your state teacher evaluation rubrics to see where aspects of global competence could help teachers demonstrate the teaching standards upon which they are already judged. You can also use these as a tool for providing feedback on teachers' global competence integration. For example, the North Carolina Professional Teaching Standards require teachers to "embrace diversity in the school community and the world," "promote global awareness and its relevance," and "make instruction relevant to students [by demonstrating] the relationship between the core content and 21st century content that includes global awareness" (Public Schools of North Carolina, 2013). Likewise, the Massachusetts Model System for Educator Evaluation includes the stipulation that each teacher "actively creates and maintains an environment in which students' diverse backgrounds, identities, strengths, and challenges are respected" (Massachusetts Department of Elementary and Secondary Education, 2018).

Collaborative Professional Community

- Take stock of the time and space already set aside for teacher collaboration. Do you have common planning times where grade levels or departments work together and provide feedback to one another? Do you have professional learning teams with specific learning-centered foci or faculty meetings with dedicated time to sharing best practices? If so, use that time to introduce global competence and allow teachers to plan for how they will integrate it into their teaching.
- If your school has yet to institute formal spaces for collaboration, start by figuring out where in your schedule you can make that happen. Take the time to institute norms for effective and professional collaboration. Once those norms and behaviors are established as a solid foundation, introduce globally competent teaching and learning as the focal point around which staff can collectively engage.

Operations and Resource Management

- Reallocate fiscal resources to support teacher planning time around the integration of global content into the curriculum. At a K–12 urban charter school in California, the school administration allocated a line in the curriculum and development budget for substitute teachers to cover classes while teachers plan. As a result, the teachers were able to develop a globalized unit of study they could implement. An elementary school leader in a Midwest town cobbled together Title I and Title II money to create two Focus Teacher positions whose job is to coach teachers on planning and modeling global lessons and help make global learning central to instruction.
- Take advantage of free opportunities for global learning. Certain online platforms that facilitate global collaboration across classrooms are free (e.g., Skype in the Classroom, Empatico). Certain fellowships for educators to travel abroad cover all the costs (e.g., National Geographic Society's Grosvenor Teacher Fellow Program, Fulbright Distinguished

Awards in Teaching Program, Fulbright Teachers for Global Classrooms Program). Some NGOs offer free webinars and classroom resources. The Smithsonian Institution has a free digital catalogue of over a million resources from its collections (www.si.edu/educators). Share these opportunities widely with your staff and encourage them to take part!

Reflection and Action

1. What funding and materials do you already have in place for global learning? Conduct an audit of the global resources you have at your school and the resources that could be reallocated toward global teaching and learning. Include the following in your audit:
   - Instructional materials (e.g., books, maps and globes, age-appropriate magazines)
   - Technology infrastructure (e.g., for participating in virtual exchanges, researching global topics)
   - Teacher collaboration time
   - Budget items (school, district, state, federal)
2. Map out the global initiatives you want to implement and the funds, materials, and time needed to get them off the ground. Based on the resources your school already has, what additional resources will you need? Where will you seek out those resources?

6

Growing Global Competence in Yourself

A good leader inspires people to have confidence in the leader. A great leader inspires people to have confidence in themselves.

Eleanor Roosevelt

"We're building the airplane as we fly." Does that sound familiar? This refrain reflects a common sentiment among principals as they discuss the state of global learning in their schools. Rarely have I met school leaders who considered themselves globally competent or global education experts prior to starting their role. Brooks and Normore (2010) likewise observed, "The near complete absence of literature connecting [glocalization] to educational leadership is troubling and suggests that it is quite possible educational leaders are unprepared to confront the realities of leading schools in a global society" (p. 54).

Delving into the unfamiliar can cause both apprehension and discomfort. It is perfectly natural to fear the unknown and uncharted territories. I was 22 years old when I strapped on my first pair of downhill skis. I dismounted from the chairlift having never taken a lesson and not entirely sure whether I could make it to the bottom of the beginner slope with all of my skis and poles intact. Of course, I had no idea how to regulate my speed and ended up zooming down the mountain at a record pace, scared out of my mind, until I intentionally tripped in an effort to stop myself from hurling into a tree, another skier, or straight into the lodge. As I watched kids no taller than my waist fly past my snow-covered self with their pom-pom hats billowing in the breeze, I felt dejected and humiliated. But my friends stopped to help me up and, despite their own ability to go down the Black Diamond routes, they stuck with me on the Green Circles all morning and taught me the basics. As the day went on, I felt more and more comfortable going down the trails and slowly reaching new heights—and letting my friends go even higher. I look back on my first day of skiing as a success because I had a team to guide me. I didn't have to go down the mountain on my own—and neither do you as you venture into leading global initiatives.

Effective leaders don't need to know all the answers. However, they to know how to surround themselves with people who do. And they know how to inspire and support others to find the answers on their own. Effective leaders demonstrate hubris by feeling comfortable falling down in front of their peers and by asking for help when they need it. There is no reason to wait to implement global initiatives until you feel completely proficient with the ins and outs of globally competent teaching and learning. You can simultaneously build capacity within yourself and among your team to bring global learning to life.

Barrier: How Can I Be a Global Leader if I Have Never Had Global Experiences Myself?

On top of everything else, school administrators are also expected to be instructional leaders focused on improving and evaluating teaching and learning. However, this becomes problematic for school leaders who are committed to providing global learning experiences but feel unqualified to lead the charge because they personally haven't spent time outside the country or with people from different cultures and backgrounds. Such leaders might ask, "How can I talk the talk if I haven't walked the walk?" The reality is that many school leaders find themselves in this situation. For those who followed the traditional pathway of getting teacher and administrator licensure through accredited preparation programs, odds are good that they did not study abroad or receive coursework that specifically covered global competence.

Colleges and schools of education remain the least internationalized on higher education campuses; few teacher education and educational leadership preparation programs offer opportunities to study and teach abroad or to learn about the international aspects of content instruction (Cushner & Brennan, 2007; Devlin-Foltz, 2010; Jean-Marie et al., 2009; Parkhouse et al., 2016). Researcher Jennifer Mahon (2010) found that only 18 percent of public institutions offering four-year baccalaureate, masters, and/or doctoral degree education programs (74 of 409) offered overseas student teaching. Data compiled by the Institute of International Education (2018) show that education was one of the least popular fields of study for students who studied abroad from 2006 to 2016. In 2016, education students accounted for only 3.3 percent of students who studied abroad, compared to 25.8 percent of students in STEM fields and 20.7 percent in business or management. Inservice training on globally competent teaching, learning, and leading is also far from ubiquitous; a survey of ASCD *SmartBrief* subscribers found that nearly 40 percent of the 1,790 administrators who responded had not received any professional development on global content (ASCD, 2016).

This dearth of teacher and educational leadership programs that integrate global competence and provide international experiences may in part contribute to school leaders and staff feeling unprepared and unsure of how to foster global competence among students. Although researchers have found that a teacher's decision to integrate global education into their instruction directly correlates with the extent to which global themes were emphasized in their teacher preparation programs and courses, few preservice teachers actually participate in such courses and experiences (Poole & Russell, 2015). The positive impact of short- and long-term study and teaching abroad programs on global competence development is also well documented. Research has found that educators who participate in overseas student teaching and cultural immersion experiences develop empathy, global mindedness, knowledge of one's own and other cultures, an understanding of the process of second language learning, skills in intercultural interactions, and an ability to adapt to student differences, work with English language learners, and apply knowledge of culture to teaching, school structures, and education systems (Mahon & Cushner, 2007; Smolcic & Katunich, 2017).

There are a few stand-out programs that offer learning opportunities explicitly for school leaders. World View, a professional development organization based out of the University of North Carolina at Chapel Hill, has offered a weeklong intensive global education leaders program for more than 15 years. This program provides K–12 and community college leaders with the opportunity to delve into global issues that affect students and to plan global programs in their schools. The North Carolina Department of Public Instruction also offers a Global Educator Digital Badge for Administrators. To be eligible for the badge, administrators must address goals that apply to global awareness elements in the North Carolina School Executive Standards, complete 100 hours of global education professional development, and complete a capstone project that demonstrates an ability to foster the school conditions for globally competent teaching to occur (North Carolina Department of Public Instruction, 2015). The U.S. Department of State's Bureau of Educational and Cultural Affairs offers exchange programs for administrators and teachers. In addition, their Fulbright Teachers for Global Classrooms Program, a yearlong opportunity for elementary, middle, and high school teachers that includes an online course, an in-person symposium, international field experience, and a capstone project, invites principals to join teachers and learn alongside them.

These examples, however, are few and far between. That is why it's not uncommon for school leaders to say, "I've never had an international experience" or "I don't know what globally competent teaching actually looks like in the classroom." A newly minted high school principal implementing a new districtwide global education initiative shared, "It can create a touch of anxiety when, as school administrators, we're supposed to be leading a professional development effort that we ourselves are not necessarily 100 percent comfortable with. School leaders, myself included, are walking lockstep with the teachers through this."

Rather than paralyzing yourself with the fear of what you do not know, embrace the challenge of taking the capacity-building journey with your teachers as you co-construct knowledge of the world and how to best engage your students and school in it.

Solution: Learn with Students, Staff, and Colleagues

Be open to expanding your worldview through personal and professional experiences. As with globally competent teaching, globally competent school leadership is not about dictating a prescribed playbook of pedagogy. School leaders who have successfully infused global learning into their schools have not done so through charismatic leadership, through dictatorial demands, or by being the single torchbearer the rest of the school blindly follows. Rather, they model a desire to learn about, from, and with the wider world and adopt democratic leadership approaches, distributing power to build personal and collective capacity to engage with the world.

Model a Learning Mindset

Actions speak louder than words. Showing a desire to continuously develop your own global competence can inspire your staff and students to do the same. Learning about the world and how to teach with the world in mind can take many forms: unpacking what global competence, global studies, or being a global school means; attending professional learning experiences focused on global competence; and the simple act of following international news stories.

Numerous school leaders whom I have interviewed studied various models and frameworks that define global competence to understand what the term truly means. Then, after reflecting on the different components of each framework and how they relate to the work in their schools, they determined whether they needed to come with a unique model or adopt an existing framework. An elementary school principal shared, "There is no project kit for global studies. Therefore, a lot of the initial work was thinking about developing our own framework of what we meant by global studies." This principal conducted his own preliminary research and intellectual thinking on what the framework might look like and then shared a draft with his staff and the district superintendent for feedback. Ultimately, the school decided on a framework that melded global citizenship with the Habits of Mind and Habits of Work the school already used when considering student learning. Their four pillars of global studies became 1) Evidence, articulating how we know something is credible; 2) Perspective, understanding differences across the globe and encouraging empathy; 3) Pattern Recognition, understanding patterns, connections, and cause-effect relationships; and 4) Relevance, answering why we should care about something and why something matters.

A middle school principal took a different approach, leading a task force of teachers and administrators that reviewed a few competing frameworks before landing on the Asia Society and CCSSO's global competence pillars: investigate the world, recognize perspectives, communicate ideas, and take action (Mansilla & Jackson, 2011). Regardless of whether you shop around to adopt an existing framework or create a definition of global competence that jives with existing approaches your school uses, this exercise of asking, "What does global competence mean?" and "Which global competence attributes are most salient to me, my staff, and students?" builds your knowledge of the construct itself and how it intersects with local conditions and concerns you deal with every day.

As you build an understanding of the global competence attributes that resonate with your school community, you can simultaneously grow your own knowledge about global conditions, events, and cultures. Jeffrey Brooks and Anthony Normore (2010) identified nine concepts of glocalization that school leaders should work toward understanding:

1. Political literacy: acting as empowered participants in political processes that influence local, national, and international decisions and

understanding the effects of globalization of education policy on one's own work.

2. Economic literacy: understanding opportunities and challenges provided by a rapidly globalizing economy so schools can best prepare students.

3. Cultural literacy: understanding that people exist in multiple cultures simultaneously and the need to balance "one global culture" with subcultures.

4. Moral literacy: understanding how to build friendship, trust, and harmony with diverse stakeholders using skills such as honesty, respect, a willingness to take responsibility, fairness, and caring.

5. Pedagogical literacy: understanding how to teach students in ways that prepare them for the world.

6. Information literacy: knowing how to prepare students for the knowledge economy, make informed judgments about what information to use, and the implications of the digital divide.

7. Organizational literacy: understanding that school leaders are change agents in the education system.

8. Spiritual and religious literacy: understanding differences and similarities regarding the spiritual and religious orientations of school stakeholders and how one's spiritual values align with one's personal and professional actions.

9. Temporal literacy: understanding the past, present, and future of people and organizations locally, nationally, and internationally.

To start to develop glocal literacy across these knowledge domains, reflect on how conditions and events around the world affect your students, the city or town where you teach, and the state or federal policies that directly affect your school.

Create your own crash courses on global understanding. Start by engaging in the simple act of following international news. Tune into or follow news outlets you ordinarily wouldn't read, listen to, or follow on social media. Pay closer attention to the World section in the news outlets you regularly follow. Listen to podcasts that address global issues on your commute to work. All these activities can open your eyes to new issues and perspectives. A high school English teacher whose class I had the pleasure of observing regularly had her students watch CNN 10 as a warm-up at the start of class. After the segment, she would ask, "Which international news stories are relevant to you and why?" Reflecting on that same question as you absorb current events can help shed light on how global issues—from water sanitation to the refugee crisis to trade wars to natural disasters—are manifesting in different communities around the world and the implications for your local school community.

Share articles, video clips, and podcasts you find particularly insightful or thought-provoking with staff. As an elementary school principal explained, "Continuing to expose my staff to things around the world provides different ways of thinking about things, and it's easy to do. I constantly send links to articles and videos to try to model curiosity about other places." When exploring and consuming news sources, be mindful of where that media is coming from and what biases that outlet might have. Ask yourself questions such as, "Who made this? Why was this made? Who might benefit or be harmed from this message? Is this fact, opinion, or propaganda? How credible is this source?" (National Association for Media Literacy Education, 2007).

Books and films that address global issues are another great medium for casually learning about different cultures, countries, the nature and consequences of globalization, and the effects of globalization. (By virtue of reading *this* book, you are already on the way there!) To enhance your learning, start a book club with colleagues or host a Friday night film screening. Figure 6.1 provides a small—and by no means comprehensive—sample of books and films that educators have found to be a helpful place to start. You can also create book clubs around texts with diverse protagonists or that address global themes your teachers plan to incorporate into the curriculum.

Before reading any book or watching any film, ask questions such as these: "What do I think I already know about this topic/country/culture? What potential biases or stereotypes might I hold about this topic/country/

Figure 6.1 | A Sample of Books and Films to Spark Global Learning

Books	• *City of Thorns: Nine Lives in the World's Largest Refugee Camp* (Ben Rawlence, 2017) • *The First 1,000 Days* (Roger Thurow, 2016) • *Globalization and Its Discontents* (Joseph E. Stiglitz, 2003) • *How Soccer Explains the World: An Unlikely Theory of Globalization* (Franklin Foer, 2010) • *The Newcomers: Finding Refuge, Friendship, and Hope in an American Classroom* (Helen Thorpe, 2017) • *The World Is Flat: A Brief History of the 21st Century* (Thomas Friedman, 2007)
Films (Documentaries)	• *Girls Rising: Changing the World One Girl at a Time* (2013) • *Plastic Paradise: The Great Pacific Garbage Patch* (2013) • *Time for School 2003–2016* (2016) • *The White Helmets* (2016) • *We Feed the World* (2005)

culture?" During and after you finish the book or film, discuss how your understanding of the topic/country/culture changed, what surprised you, what made you think or understand something from a different perspective, and potential implications for students, your school, the curriculum, and instruction in general. Rich conversations such as this will help you build an appreciation for and complex understanding of the vast array of global issues while making connections both to similar issues your students might be facing and to curricular content.

Formalize your own education on global issues and perspectives, and infuse them into your school culture, curriculum, and instruction. Online learning opportunities abound (e.g., the World Savvy Global Competence Certificate, ASCD Streaming videos on globally competent teaching, and Primary Source webinars and videos on a host of global topics). Local universities may offer courses and institutes as part of their international and global studies programs or through Title VI National Resource Centers, which provide instruction, research, training, and materials. Your willingness to learn and grow can rub off on the teachers around you, which in turn can motivate students.

Globally competent school leaders rarely travel solo on their learning journeys. Rather than learn alone, leaders surround themselves with a network of colleagues at their school—and far beyond—to provide support and camaraderie in what can be daunting work. In addition to enlisting peers around your building, try to build a network of globally minded educators across your district and geographic boundaries. Learning is a social process (Vygotsky, 1978), and networks are a powerful tool for processing new information, giving you new ideas, and providing critical feedback on your practice (Bryk, Gomez, Grunow, & LeMahieu, 2015; Coburn & Russell, 2008; Trust, 2012).

There's no shortage of ways to build your network. School leaders I've interviewed have built their networks in different ways. Some connect with educators and forge relationships with the people they meet overseas, on formal exchange trips or personal travels. Others attend conferences and symposia within the United States where they network with speakers and other educators. Still other leaders reach out to nearby districts to learn how schools with similar demographics have implemented global initiatives. Others also serve as a mentor, opening their school as an exemplar for others; partner with organizations that provide global professional development and help forge connections between partner schools; or create virtual networks that traverse the globe, using social media to create and sustain connections. Although there is no prescribed way to build a global professional learning network, common across all these examples is that you must put yourself out there in the world. This sets a powerful example for the staff around you to do the same.

Embrace Collaborative Leadership

Without fail, globally competent school leaders adopt a collaborative leadership style that gives staff voice and choice in designing and implementing global initiatives. Analogous to shared leadership (Wahlstrom & Louis, 2008), participatory leadership (Tichnor-Wagner, Harrison, & Cohen-Vogel, 2016), or distributed leadership (Spillane, 2005), collaborative leadership gives teachers influence over decision making at the school and classroom levels. This style of leadership has been associated with positive outcomes related to school climate and improvements to teaching practices and student achievement (Marks & Printy, 2003; Wahlstrom & Louis, 2008).

Creating a democratic school culture that ensures teachers have the space to start initiatives from the ground up is key to getting global learning off the ground (Lindsay, 2016; Wiley, 2013). From a managerial standpoint, this gives teachers ownership over decisions about how to incorporate your school's global competence framework, which can result in deeper and more sustained levels of implementation (Coburn, 2003). From a practical standpoint, a collaborative leadership structure takes the pressure off you so you're less likely to feel like you must develop global competence expertise before asking your staff and students to do the same. Instead of fretting about knowing the ins and outs of globally competent teaching, use your energy to create an environment in which professional learning and student learning are in teachers' hands. Creating such an environment involves a shift in mindset, the creation of tangible structures for collaboration, room for differentiation and experimentation, and the inclusion of student voice.

Shift the leadership mindset. Globally competent leaders reject a top-down managerial approach that dictates what globally competent teaching must look like. They also reject a "Great Man" or "heroics of leadership" mentality wherein one leader swoops in to singlehandedly turn a school around. Instead, they adopt an image of themselves as facilitators and cheerleaders who enable teachers to implement their own ideas. This gives motivated teachers permission to pursue their passions and teacher-led initiatives the freedom to grow and spread. As a middle school principal observed, "Teachers are happy to have the freedom to go deep when you give them permission."

Globally competent leaders have described their role as a simple one: say *yes* (within reason) to global initiatives that teachers want to pursue, whether it's a request to apply for a Fulbright Fellowship, start a schoolwide project on a global issue, bring in a guest speaker on a global topic, or create a partnership with a school overseas. Indeed, multiple principals of globally focused schools have readily admitted that a teacher first introduced them to the very concept of global education.

Examples abound of powerful teacher-led initiatives in the global education space. In Seattle Public Schools, teachers were the driving force behind the district's vision for global education and the ongoing capacity building of the district's ten international schools (Zeichner, 2015). Seattle Public Schools' International Schools Leadership Team (ISLT) is composed of teacher leaders dedicated to building capacity at their respective schools and fostering global citizens via cultural and global competence, global perspectives, and world languages. In Illinois, a Fulbright Teachers for Global Classrooms alum led a group of teachers to successfully initiate the statewide Illinois Global Scholar Certificate program. The Global Read-Aloud program began as a simple way to connect one teacher's classroom with classrooms around the world as they read the same book over the same six-week period. The project has since grown from 150 students in 2010 to more than one million kids today. (For more information, visit theglobalreadaloud.com.)

Of course, if teachers are to feel comfortable and confident jumping into the driver's seat and steering the direction of globally competent teaching and learning, there needs to be a mindset shift. Leaders can actively cultivate this shift through constant encouragement and trusting that teachers will do the work well, even if they don't know how a project will turn out.

School administrators whom I have interviewed, regardless of whether they introduced global education to their schools or jumped on a bandwagon driven by an enthusiastic teacher, have stressed the importance of giving teachers independence in how they incorporate global competence into their classrooms. They allow teachers to figure it out for themselves in ways that make the most sense for their students and content. The beauty of global learning is that it can—and should—look different in different classrooms. When I visited elementary and high schools focused on global studies in

Washington, DC, I was amazed to see how teachers covering vastly different content and teaching students as young as 5 and as old as 17 picked up and ran with Project Zero's Global Thinking Routines (Mansilla, 2016). A kindergarten teacher had her students use photos to "see, think, and wonder" and make connections between garbage collection in their own city and around the world as part of a unit on community helpers. A 9th grade science teacher used the same global thinking routine, calling on students to "see, think, and wonder" about images of a produce market in Turkey and of deforestation, and prompted students to ask where food comes from, how it is distributed in different parts of the world, and how food supplies might be threatened—all as an introduction to a unit on photosynthesis. Across town, a biology teacher took a different approach to integrating global learning and chose to engage her students in an interdisciplinary investigation into infectious diseases, where students examined viruses from scientific, mathematical, political, and cultural perspectives and shared their findings with the broader community.

In addition to classroom-level decisions, school administrators should give teachers autonomy in making school-level decisions around globally competent teaching: from which courses are offered to school events to schoolwide projects. For example, a middle school principal in a small city shared how one teacher created her own global dance class as an elective because that was her passion and background. A K–8 magnet school principal instituted a rotating committee of three grade-level teams who determined a monthly global theme and specific learning activities for the entire student body. As teachers find creative ways to bring global issues and perspectives into their classrooms and schools, you too will expand your knowledge of what global learning looks like and what tends to work best.

There will, undoubtedly, be times when you have to say *no*. Either the budget simply won't allow for an idea or a teacher ventures a little too far off course from his or her content area. For example, one elementary school principal shared how he had to turn down a teacher requesting funds for a learning program in the Galapagos because the costs were too high. Another suburban middle school principal had to remind one particularly passionate global educator that she still had an obligation to teach specific standards within the scope and sequence of her language curriculum while addressing social justice–oriented global issues. This principal equated collaborative leadership to that of a gardener:

> It models what global citizenship is—grassroots change that percolates upward. You're a gardener that lets it grow. Having teachers grow things works better than telling teachers what to do. Sometimes you have to prune and say hard things and scaffold so that the idea will end up being successful and sustainable in the long run. Sometimes you don't know what's going to happen when you plant the seeds. For all deep teaching and learning, that's how you want to grow things.

Make professional collaboration space. Globally competent school leaders create several formal spaces for collaboration around global competence to occur. Research and practical experience bear out the importance of scheduling collaborative planning time so teachers can form strong professional communities (Louis, Marks, & Kruse, 1996; Tichnor-Wagner, Harrison, & Cohen-Vogel, 2016; Wahlstrom & Louis, 2008). Examples include grade-level, content-area, or cross-departmental PLCs; small learning teams that collaborate around common students; instructional leadership teams with teacher leaders from each subject area; morning collaboratives; weekly professional learning communities; collaborative professional development sessions after school; and summer institutes.

Whether you refer to them as communities of practice, professional learning communities, or professional learning teams, successful collaborative spaces—those spaces that result in real changes to teacher practice and student outcomes—include the following ingredients (Little, 2002; McLaughlin & Talbert, 2001):

- Shared vision toward student learning.
- Commitment to taking up new practices that benefit student learning.
- Connection to classroom practice.

- Supportive community (e.g., through codeveloping lesson plans or units, sharing best practices, allowing opportunities for teachers to observe one another).

Collaborative communities focused on globally competent teaching and learning have a shared vision of fostering global competence among students, hold an expectation that teachers will infuse globally competent teaching practices into their instruction, and give teachers time to collaboratively map globally competent teaching elements onto existing units within their content areas, implement those lessons and units, and reflect on how those lessons went.

These collaborative spaces might already exist in your school. If not, your role as a leader is to institute them and create a foundation on which capacity for fostering global competence can grow. If these spaces already exist, allocate time for global professional learning to occur. A majority of school leaders whom I have interviewed didn't see themselves as global competence experts. They left that role to teachers or external professional development providers. Instead, leaders provided the basic tools, materials, and access to technical support that teachers could use to design global learning experiences in the direction they desired.

For example, a chief academic officer at an urban K–12 charter school shared that he asked early adopters to model what global integration looked like for their fellow teachers, from unit mapping to the creation of essential questions to classroom implementation. An elementary school principal explained how he set the expectations and norms for staff to use the designated professional learning time to discuss their planning and introduced protocols for how teachers could share their work and structure their conversations. He then left the bulk of the time for teachers to collaborate with one another on global project planning. At the end of these collaborative planning sessions, he would ask, "What support do you need next?" A middle school principal likewise took time at the beginning of the school year to introduce the school's global competence framework to the entire staff and then had his staff break up into content- and grade-level teams during com-mon planning time to determine how they would use the framework as a guidepost for enhancing or changing their curriculum. At the end of the year, each team would reflect on what worked effectively and what elements and topics should be moved to different units.

Numerous school leaders whom I have interviewed implement multiple ways for teachers to engage in collaborative learning activities around global competence. For example, an elementary school principal used Title I fund-ing for a summer institute focused on global project-based learning that all staff attended. He then devoted delayed openings in his district for teach-ers to dive deeply into project planning and receive peer feedback on their projects and lesson planning guides. A middle school principal used exist-ing common planning times, monthly professional learning teams focused on problems of practice, department meetings, and faculty meetings to give teachers an opportunity to understand the school's global competence frame-work and how to use it to enhance their curriculum. A high school principal set aside dedicated time to share ideas and innovate around global learning during faculty meetings, summer professional development, monthly PLCs, and monthly morning collaboratives. In short, multiple, structured touch-points for professional collaboration leads to a spiraling presence of global learning throughout the year—for both teachers and students.

Allow for differentiation and experimentation. Teachers at your school may vary widely in the amount of exposure they have had to diverse cultures and countries, how globally connected they feel, and in how comfortable they are teaching for global competence. Some may have extensive experience traveling abroad and immersing themselves in new cultures; others may have not ventured outside their home state or have never found reason to leave the homogenous communities in which they grew up. Some may already pay attention to international current events and easily make connections to their lessons; others may not. This makes differentiation incredibly important.

For teachers who do not consider themselves globally aware, lead-ers should take baby steps to arrive at deep and lasting change to teaching practice. As one rural elementary school principal explained to me, "The biggest thing is to start small. Change one thing first, then add something else, and then add something else." For example, set an expectation for teachers to complete one lesson plan that connects to a global issue. As they become more confident in connecting the content to their classroom instruction, increase the number of globally focused lessons they plan. By contrast, more experienced teachers may integrate global competence across multiple units or create interdisciplinary units in which students use project-based learning approaches to investigate a global issue.

Leaders with experienced and passionate global educators can further differentiate by tapping them to run professional learning communities or to coach less experienced peers. The chief academic officer at an urban K–12 charter school explained how his school adopted a "train the trainer" mentality to differentiate professional learning. Veteran teachers from each content area experienced in integrating the school's global competence model joined a "mentorship" cohort and, with the support of a coach, became the coaches who trained teachers just beginning this type of work.

The Globally Competent Learning Continuum (GCLC, https://global-learning.ascd.org) is a free, validated, online self-reflection tool you can use with your staff to determine where your school is starting from. The GCLC breaks down the 12 elements of globally competent teaching (see Chapter 1) into five developmental levels: nascent, beginning, progressing, proficient, and advanced. For each element, teachers self-reflect on how they would rate themselves based on personal and professional experiences. Even if you aren't leading from the classroom, you can personally reflect on these elements and ask yourself, "How do I already provide support for teachers in developing this element? In what ways can I provide more support?"

After teachers individually self-reflect, as a staff or in small cohorts share specific areas of strength and areas for improvement. (See Figure 6.2 for steps to guide you.) This will allow you to pinpoint areas where you can collectively focus professional development, coaching, or curricular resources or areas where some teachers may be able to mentor others (Tichnor-Wagner et

Figure 6.2 | Using the Globally Competent Learning Continuum to Guide Global PLCs

The Globally Competent Learning Continuum (GCLC, globallearning.ascd.org) provides 12 concrete globally competent teaching elements with descriptions of what each looks like at different development levels. If you are a facilitator of an educator team or an administrator leading a schoolwide effort to incorporate global competence into students' education, follow the steps below to collectively assess your team's global competence.

1. Self-reflect individually. Ask team members to individually read through the descriptions of nascent, beginning, progressing, proficient, and advanced for each element of the GCLC and independently select the level for each element that best describes them. Then have them identify the professional and personal experiences or practices that led them to make that choice.

2. Identify areas for team improvement. Ask team members to share elements in which they rated themselves highly and those in which they rated themselves as nascent, beginning, or progressing. (Because the elements include sensitive topics, do not require individuals to share aloud if that makes them uncomfortable.) Select one or two elements on which to focus team improvement that best fits your collective needs. Set a group goal outlining how you plan to improve in the element(s) you selected as your goal.

3. Take action. Select one or more professional learning experiences to help you reach your goal (e.g., reading a series of articles or books, convening a book study, enrolling in an online course, attending a conference, signing up for an overseas teaching experience, designing and implementing a new lesson or unit). Note the timeline for when your team will start and complete these experiences, and then follow through on that plan.

4. Reevaluate your level. After you complete Step 3, reconvene as a group and repeat Step 1.

Source: Adapted from *The Globally Competent Learning Continuum Facilitator Guide*, by ASCD myTeachSource, 2017.

al., 2019). Be mindful not to use the GCLC as an evaluative measure. Global competence includes sensitive topics, and educators need to be in a nonjudgmental space to provide an honest and accurate assessment of where they are on their global learning journey.

Along that same nonjudgmental vein, embrace innovation through a "freedom to fail" mentality. Encourage teachers to experiment and test new ideas that might not work as planned or go in a different direction than they originally intended. Rather than focus on fidelity to outcomes, guide teachers to engage in reflective inquiry that asks the following questions:

1. What are the aims of the lesson, project, or unit that I tested?
2. Did the lesson, project, or unit reach the desired outcome?
3. What processes, activities, or resources helped or hindered the success of this lesson, project, or unit?
4. Would I teach this lesson, project, or unit again? If so, what modifications might I make? If not, why will I discard it?

As you support teachers through reflective learning cycles, you too will increase your own understanding of what effective global learning looks like in different classrooms, grade levels, and subject areas.

Encourage student-led learning. Don't limit leadership to teachers. The more advanced levels of globally competent teaching let students lead their own learning, be it through interdisciplinary inquiries on global issues, intercultural conversations, or forming and maintaining partnerships to develop their own authentic global learning opportunities (Tichnor-Wagner et al., 2019). The same can be true for schoolwide initiatives. If students are interested in starting a club focused on the environment or international films, give them the green light (and sign on to be their sponsor!). If students want to start a schoolwide fundraiser for a natural disaster affecting a community they care about, provide them with all the structural support they will need. A middle school principal shared how a student whose family had a Russian background approached him, saying he wanted to learn Russian. At first, the principal's response was, "I'm not sure how to help you but let me think about it." With no world language staff qualified to teach Russian and not enough interested students to fill a class, he ended up buying commercial language-learning software for the student—who ultimately pursued an independent study of Russian for three years at the school. As the principal pointed out, "This could be a pathway that leads him to a course of study in college that he really loves."

Middle and high school capstone projects are another powerful way for students to pursue global topics in which they are personally interested and invested. Though there is not a universal global competence capstone project template, they tend to do three things:

1. Allow students to explore a glocal issue they deem important.
2. Ask students to investigate a viewpoint from multiple perspectives and communicate with real stakeholders during the process.
3. Prompt students to recommend actions for improving that issue.

Provide opportunities for students to present their projects to the broader school community (e.g., a schoolwide assembly or global fair) so you, their peers, their teachers, and their families can learn about or gain a new perspective on a global issue. You will quickly realize that your students are the content experts who can teach you about the issues they investigated.

Renowned global education scholar Fernando Reimers (2009b) sums up why collaborative leadership is a critical ingredient to advancing global learning in schools:

> An organized, bottom-up, teacher-led movement can advance global education in ways that advocates have been unable to do so far. . . . Let us follow, recognize, and support teachers and students as they discover together how best to prepare the next generation for global civility and international understanding. Their shared work in the classroom is the most powerful driver we have in achieving these ambitious education goals. (paras. 26, 28)

Actions to Grow Global Competence in Yourself

The following are some concrete examples of how to apply the following globally competent leadership skills as you embark on your personal journey of global competence development alongside your students, staff, and broader school community:

- Facilitating a shared mission and vision.
- Supporting curriculum, instruction, and assessment.
- Fostering a collaborative professional community.
- Connecting and collaborating globally.
- Striving for equity and inclusivity.

Shared Mission and Vision

- Learn about what global competence means from the perspective of students, staff, and community members. In addition to exploring published frameworks that define global competence, ask students, parents, community members, and teachers about the knowledge, skills, and mindsets they think are important to thrive in today's world and about the global issues they feel are important to solve.

Curriculum, Instruction, and Assessment

- Create formal processes for students to propose schoolwide service projects that address glocal issues. For example, an elementary school teacher in a Title I school in the Southeast encouraged students to propose service projects by having them write a proposal and set up a meeting with her to discuss the project, how they developed the idea, and why they want to pursue it. Students as young as 7 years old went to her office and organized projects to raise awareness about the food crisis in Venezuela, petition for WIC stamps to cover organic food in the local grocery store, and fundraise for a cleft palette society to finance surgeries overseas. The principal shared how these project ideas often emerged from topics the students were exploring in class and introduced her to new topics and organizations.

Collaborative Professional Community

- Create opportunities for cross-departmental and grade-level pollination to occur. A middle school principal explained how he incorporated elective teachers into department PLCs, which helped all teachers see their lessons from different perspectives, find solutions to problems of practice related to global learning, and create interdisciplinary units. During district-allocated teacher workdays, he also provided times for teachers to share their global units and strategies with PLCs in different content areas (e.g., bringing the math and science PLCs together.) This helped teachers get new ideas about how to incorporate global issues they could tweak for their own content areas.

- Elevate teachers as leaders. This can take the form of formal positions, such as membership on a school leadership team or global advisory group that oversees school global efforts. One suburban high school principal created a Faculty Citizens of the World group, which met monthly to work on making the school more globally aware. Beyond formal leadership structures, school leaders should hand teachers the keys to leading initiatives they are passionate about and put teachers forward as global citizenship exemplars by celebrating global initiatives they are leading in newsletters, on social media, and during community events. For example, the first year that his school incorporated global competence into its mission and vision, a high school principal sent one of his teachers to the state history conference to find inspiration for innovative global initiatives. The teacher returned with the idea to organize a festival wherein each student would partake in an inquiry-based project focused on finding creative solutions to social problems faced by developing countries. Teachers across departments came together to design and implement the project. As the principal shared,

"A teacher leader took ownership. It was a learning stretch for the kids, the teachers, and the principal" (Tichnor-Wagner, 2019, p. 11).

- Multiple times throughout the year, take the pulse of teachers' learning needs in order to identify their strengths and needs, areas for professional growth, and an action plan for improvement. For example, have staff use the GCLC to self-assess on the 12 elements of globally competent teaching. Write each element on chart paper and ask staff to put a green sticker beside areas where they rated themselves as proficient or advanced and yellow stickers for where they rated themselves as nascent or beginning. Use these data "stickers" to tailor professional learning activities to staff's actual needs.

Global Connections and Collaborations

- Go out into the world! Seek out opportunities for educational leaders to travel. EF International, World View, and the U.S. Department of State all offer exchange programs specifically geared toward school leaders. If your school or district offers exchange programs for students, request to serve as a chaperone on one.
- Join online platforms to connect with educators across different boundaries. Twitter, Facebook, Edmodo, and Ning are just a handful of platforms that educators use to interact with a broad professional learning network. (And as sure as technology changes, I imagine the list of platforms will too.) These platforms allow educators to stay up to date on education research, articles, policy, and news; post questions and answers on problems of practice; and crowdsource curricular and instructional resources (Trust, 2012).
- There is no need to reinvent the wheel. Form partnerships with outside vendors who can provide the tools and training you need to integrate global learning. Be in constant communication with them, help with the management side of the partnership, and participate in learning activities alongside your staff. The latter will further buoy the will of your staff to engage because they see you as an active learner.

Equity and Inclusivity

- Learn from the diversity within your school community. For example, survey the languages that students speak at home, and use that as a springboard for learning simple phrases to engage with families and make students feel more comfortable. Utilize a "funds of knowledge" approach for home visits at the beginning of the school year by studying the "culturally accumulated bodies of knowledge and skills" within students' homes, such as home language, values and traditions, caregiving, family occupations, and educational activities (Moll, Amanti, Neff, & Gonzalez, 1992, p. 133). Ensure that opportunities for parent involvement are accessible to families of all cultural, linguistic, and socioeconomic backgrounds, and feature parents of diverse backgrounds as guest speakers, advocates, and program participants (Barbian, Gonzalez, & Mejia, 2017).

- As you interact with students and families who come from a culture that differs from yours, refrain from imposing your own cultural norms, values, traditions, and beliefs. Instead, use it as a learning opportunity to build cultural literacy. This begins by reflecting on your own culture as a gateway to understanding the similarities and differences in the cultures of those you interact with across your school community.

Reflection and Action

1. What previous knowledge and experiences have increased your knowledge of diverse perspectives, cultures, and languages; globalization and global issues; and how to incorporate this knowledge into classroom instruction and schoolwide programming? Which of these areas do you need to learn more about? What new learning activities will you use to increase your knowledge and skills in those areas?

2. What type of leadership structure do you or does your school currently embrace: a top-down chain of command, a collaborative approach, or something in the middle? How can you create more formal and informal opportunities that allow for teacher and student leadership in global initiatives?

Globally Competent Leadership Throughout the System

The world's not going to change unless we are willing to change ourselves.

Rigoberta Menchu

School leaders are crucial catalysts for successfully bringing instructional initiatives to life and sustaining those initiatives for long-term impact. To do so, they broker competing policy demands and weave them into a clear vision for the entire school community, generate will among diverse school stakeholders, find resources to support implementation, and create collective capacity of all staff. As the previous chapters illustrate, globally competent teaching practices and schoolwide programming face significant barriers to implementation. Therefore, globally competent school leadership is crucial for turning schools into relevant spaces for learning in today's diverse, interconnected world.

Bishop (1990) argued that books must serve as both windows into new worlds and mirrors that reflect who students already are. Taking this metaphor a step further, I argue that the entire school community must serve as windows and mirrors so students become engaged in their learning and feel prepared and excited for the future. For schools to become those windows and mirrors, school leaders must embrace change at three levels: self, school, and systems.

Self Change

Globally competent leaders build the infrastructure and unlock the doors for students and staff to develop global competence—and through that process become more globally competent themselves. What is exciting about this approach is that you don't already need to possess the attributes of global competence to be a globally competent leader. For example, you might not know how to communicate in more than one language, feel like you have a firm grasp on the effects of globalization on local economies, or have taken actions to solve a global issue. Globally competent school leaders lead *with* teachers, students, and community members in a quest to understand the world and transform it into a more equitable, just, sustainable place.

Over time, your practices and actions will hopefully change your own self-perception. As you align initiatives and contextual needs, garner will, find resources, and build capacity for globally competent teaching and learning at your school, you may find yourself developing the very attributes you're aiming to develop among students, such as empathy, perspective recognition, knowledge of global conditions and current events, ability to communicate and collaborate with people from diverse backgrounds, and a desire to take action on issues of local and global importance.

You may develop empathy and perspective recognition as you actively listen to stakeholders' concerns while garnering political will, particularly those stakeholders who disagree with you about the value of global competence. You may gain knowledge of global issues and their local manifestations as you conduct research on the alignment between the global initiatives you plan to roll out and the existing needs of the school community. You may improve your intercultural communication and collaboration skills as you welcome families from culturally and linguistically diverse backgrounds into the school community and as partners in student learning. You may decide to reduce your own carbon footprint after hearing students present ideas for combatting the effects of climate change.

Finally, by virtue of following through on the implementation actions described in the preceding chapters, you are taking action on an issue of local and global importance: transforming education systems so they are rigorous and relevant. In short, becoming a globally competent school leader culminates in the development of effective leadership practices that lead to positive changes in teaching and learning and the very attributes we aspire to see in our students.

School Change

Transforming schools is no easy process. Schools are complex organisms. To truly transform schools into places of relevant, real-world learning, we must change a number of things: teachers' understanding of content and how students learn; teaching practices and learning activities in which students engage; the school culture and climate, including expectations and goals for student learning, how staff communicate and collaborate with one another, and the decision-making process; and the physical space in which learning takes place (Elmore, 1996; Tichnor-Wagner, Harrison, & Cohen-Vogel, 2016).

As such, changing schools into places of global learning is a holistic endeavor. To illustrate this point, Primary Source's Building Global Schools Toolkit identifies four elements of a global school: curriculum, institutional practices, professional development, and school culture (Primary Source, 2017). Likewise, the Global School Design Model, utilized by Asia Society's International Studies Schools Network, includes vision, mission and culture, student learning outcomes, organization and governance, partnerships, professional development, and curriculum, instruction, and assessment (Asia Society, n.d.).

School change also involves everyone: students, teachers, support staff, school administrators, families, and community members. A common thread among the principals interviewed for the ASCD and Longview Foundation Globally Competent Educational Leadership whitepaper was that they all engaged a wide range of stakeholders as they infused global competence across different school domains (Tichnor-Wagner & Manise, 2019). For example, school leaders brought in teachers, district leaders, and students to develop a shared definition of global competence; provided opportunities for teachers and external organizations to lead global competence professional development; and invited families, local businesses, universities, and other community organizations to contribute to global learning activities in which students were engaged.

This holistic approach is about changing hearts and minds—along with changing behaviors. Rather than simply asking teachers to comply with their demands, leaders give ownership to staff over what globally competent teaching and learning should look like. Giving ownership—knowledge of what a reform entails and the authority to make decisions about what and how that reform should be taught—to those who will actually bring it to students may lead to greater sustainability and growth (Coburn, 2003). Therefore, true school transformation is not just the physical and observable manifestation of lesson plans that integrate global content or weekly virtual exchanges with a partner school. It is a mentality wherein school staff and students believe global competence to be a worthy and vital outcome to pursue.

School change also takes time. As with any school reform, change doesn't happen overnight. Many school and district leaders recommend giving yourself at least a year to plan implementation and build will among key stakeholders (Tichnor-Wagner, 2016; Tichnor-Wagner & Manise, 2019). Then give yourself a year or two to support teachers as they change their teaching practices and another year or two after that before you can expect to see measurable changes in student outcomes. This practical wisdom is reinforced by research, which finds that it can take five to ten years for full implementation of new reforms to take root and outcomes to be observed (Cheung & Wong, 2011; Desimone, 2002). As a school administrator from Los Angeles shared, "You're going to take five years until you see fruits of labor pay off. That's hard to swallow when we want to see immediate results. But that's not the best way to look at global competence at all. It's a process of student learning over time."

Despite all this advice, if there's one constant about schools, it's change. The irony is that all this change makes schools feel static. A revolving door of reforms can rightfully cause educators to brush aside what they perceive to be the flavor of the week. If a new program is here today and gone tomorrow, then is it really worth the time and headache of figuring out? With that in mind, when coming up with a game plan for infusing global competence into your school, commit to at least three to five years of planning—and communicate that commitment!

Finally, it is important to measure the effect of the changes you are making. If you don't measure your results, how do you know if you're making improvements? How will you know when you have succeeded?

Assessing global competence can be difficult to do, given that current accountability systems don't measure it. Indeed, you could argue that end-of-year state tests are antithetical to global competence development. The very structure of multiple-choice tests—the standard structure for many state accountability regimes—does not make room for different perspectives. Students are judged based on whether they select the one "right" answer, and they do not have the space to express the rationale for how they arrived at their conclusions. Overwhelmingly, the subject areas stressed by high-stakes testing continue to be math, reading, and science. Even with the passage of the Every Student Succeeds Act, which requires states to include a nonacademic indicator, a majority of states have selected chronic absenteeism and college-and-career-readiness measures (e.g., SAT scores, ACT scores, AP/IB credit, CTE credits, industry credentials) rather than socioemotional indicators that overlap with global competence attributes (Jordan & Marley, 2018).

Global competence is certainly a means to achieving distal outcomes, such as academic achievement and reducing chronic absenteeism. Yet it is equally important to measure global competence as an outcome unto itself. What we measure in schools sends a message about what we value. And if we don't measure global competence, there is no way to know whether the global initiatives we've brought to our schools are leading to changes in teacher practice (e.g., integrating global perspectives and content into traditional subject areas, facilitating student investigations of glocal issues, forging partnerships with classrooms in different countries) or resulting in changes in how students engage in the classroom and beyond.

Practical measures—for example, surveys, observation checklists, and focus groups—are a helpful tool for getting quick formative data on your school's global competence goals since they are embedded into the regular work of schools and produce data in a timely manner (Bryk et al., 2015). Some of these tools might already exist. For example, your school climate survey might include questions about whether students feel cared for and valued and whether parents feel welcome in the school. Other tools you may need to create. Regardless, whatever you measure should align to the global competence goals stated in your school mission and vision and should be agreed upon by stakeholders throughout your school community.

For example, to measure changes in teacher practice, you could use the GCLC as a self-reflection tool for staff and track changes in how they rate themselves on different elements over time. You could also conduct regular walkthroughs with an observation protocol, looking for examples of globally competent teaching. Are global issues, content, and perspectives integrated into the lesson? Are students engaged in intercultural conversations? Are students discussing multiple perspectives around an issue? Are students asking questions about local and global issues and current events? Figure 7.1 provides an observation checklist of globally competent teaching in action. When conducting observations, keep in mind that you shouldn't expect to see every element of globally competent teaching in a single lesson, but a handful of elements at a time.

Analyzing student work with small groups of teachers can also provide insights into the depth of learning taking place. Conduct interviews and focus groups with teachers and students, asking them to share specific global learning activities they've participated in and the effect they've had. Finally, you can analyze patterns of participation. How many students are enrolled in global studies courses, dual immersion programs, and global competence certificate programs? How many classrooms are engaging students in

Figure 7.1 | Globally Competent Teaching Observation Checklist

Empathy and Valuing Multiple Perspectives	
	Multiple viewpoints or perspectives on a given topic, event, country, etc. are shared.
	Teacher and/or students discuss what has shaped their and others' beliefs or perspectives.
	Teacher and/or students are encouraged to take on viewpoints that they might not agree with.
Commitment to Promoting Equity Worldwide	
	Specific global inequities are discussed.
	The root causes of specific global inequities are discussed.
	Students take real action to address inequities.
Understanding of Global Conditions and Current Events	
	Maps are displayed and referenced.
	Local and/or global current events are read and/or discussed.
	Rationale behind local and global conditions and events are discussed.
Understanding of the Ways the World is Interconnected	
	How the local community is globally connected is examined.
	How teacher and/or students are globally connected is discussed.
	Positive and/or negative consequences of globalization are discussed.
Experiential Understanding of Multiple Cultures	
	Teacher and/or students reflect on their cultural norms.
	Teacher brings diverse cultural perspectives into the classroom (e.g., through books, film, presenters).
	Teacher and/or students share and reflect on cultural experiences they have had.
Understanding of Intercultural Communication	
	Teacher discusses multilingualism in positive terms.
	Students talk to one another in languages they feel comfortable using.
	Teachers use nonverbal communication cues.
Communicate in Multiple Languages	
	Multiple languages are visibly posted or written around the classroom.
	Teacher uses words and phrases from students' home language.
	Bilingual books and texts are present in the classroom.
Create a Classroom Environment that Values Diversity and Global Engagement	
	Students share beliefs, knowledge, skills, and practices from their home culture.

	Controversial topics are discussed and multiple viewpoints are shared respectfully.
	Classroom resources (e.g., decorations, books) represent different cultures and countries.
Integrate Learning Experiences for Students that Promote Content-Aligned Explorations of the World	
	Global content and perspectives are integrated into lessons on subject-area standards.
	Students engage in inquiry-based learning (e.g., project-based learning, design challenge).
	Students engage in interdisciplinary learning activities.
Facilitate Intercultural and International Conversations that Promote Active Listening, Critical Thinking, and Perspective Recognition	
	Students converse with people from different cultural backgrounds (e.g., via video-chat, online posts, guest speakers).
	Teacher and students model active listening skills during conversations.
Develop Local, National, and International Partnerships that Provide Real-World Contexts for Global Learning Opportunities	
	Lesson/unit/project involves a partner organization or classroom from outside the school.
	Lesson/unit/project with partner has structured learning outcomes.
	Teacher and students have engaged with or plan to engage with partner multiple times.
Develop and Use Appropriate Methods of Inquiry to Assess Students' Global Competence Development	
	Lesson objectives aligned to a specific global competence attribute are clearly articulated.
	Teacher uses formative (e.g., exit slip, checklist, reflective journal entry) or summative (e.g., report, presentation) assessment that clearly measure global competence attributes.
	Teacher modifies global instruction based on assessment results.

Note: This checklist is based on the elements of globally competent teaching as presented in *Becoming a Globally Competent Teacher* (Tichnor-Wagner, Parkhouse, Glazier, & Cain, 2019).

project-based learning activities where they are researching solutions to global problems? Utilizing a mix of measures can help you assess 1) deep changes to teacher beliefs, how teachers engage with students in the classroom, and how teachers and students engage in instructional materials, and 2) the spread of globally competent teaching and learning to more classrooms and students (Coburn, 2003).

Systems Change

Schools are not the only place for leaders to exert influence in an effort to support students' global competence development. Schools are nested in the larger education system comprised of districts, states, and the federal government—a system that is itself influenced by external organizations, institutions, and public opinion. School leaders can flex their advocacy muscles to promote policies across the systems that support global learning in schools. Indeed, school leaders may be the best people to do it because they have the on-the-ground knowledge of contextual requirements for and constraints to putting new ideas to practice.

Each level of this larger system has jurisdiction over different aspects of education. District leadership, including the superintendent, school board members, and central office administrators, approve curriculum, allocate funding and time for instructional materials and professional development, and determine policies for field trips and out-of-school activities. State governments, which include state boards of education, departments of education, governors, and state legislators, determine curricular standards, student assessments, graduation requirements, teacher licensure programs, and teacher evaluations—all of which are tied into accountability systems based on federal guidelines and approval (Cooper & Fusarelli, 2009). State budgets also account for nearly half of school funding, with the remainder coming from local revenue (Leachman & Figueroa, 2019).

Schools of education also play an integral role in preparing globally competent teachers and leaders (Tichnor-Wagner et al., 2019). Teacher and leadership preparation programs operate semiautonomously from the education governance system as they train educators to lead classrooms and schools. Even though they are beholden to state laws for licensure requirements and approvals for courses of study, they generally have autonomy over how programs are structured and the learning activities that students experience. Higher education institutions remain the primary trainer of teachers. Traditional teacher preparation programs in schools of education account for 70 percent of all teacher preparation programs in the United States, and two-thirds of alternative teacher education routes are also housed at higher education institutions (Kuenzi, 2018).

In addition to training the next generation of educators with a global mindset, universities can provide in-service professional development, through faculty programs, grants, or centers. For example, Kent State University led a Global Leadership Innovation Institute that convened university faculty and leaders from local schools. The University of North Carolina at Chapel Hill is home to World View, a public service program that has partnerships with over 145 districts and schools and provides global professional development to K–12 schools and community colleges across the state.

The following sections include examples of district, state, and higher education policies that globally committed practitioners have identified as important to supporting school and self-transformation.

District Policies

Districts can align resources around global teaching and learning. For example, they can form partnerships with external organizations that provide professional development, offset the school-level costs of professional development or IB certification, ensure the technology infrastructure exists for virtual connections, and assign district personnel to oversee global initiatives and provide technical support to schools. District leadership also sets policies regarding international travel for students, without which face-to-face exchange is impossible, and provides official approval to schools that want to participate in exchange programs, adopt global themes, or introduce new courses.

State Policies

State governments can integrate global competence outcomes into their standard course of study and teacher evaluations. Putting global competence into the accountability system sends a clear signal that knowledge, skills, and dispositions matter and need to be taught.

State governments can also utilize capacity-building tools to support school-level implementation of global initiatives. For example, they can provide a budget line for grants that fund professional training or support external organizations that can serve as global learning hubs and coordinate global competence resources. States can also create recognition systems for students, teachers, schools, and districts that provide guideposts for what global-ready students, educators, schools, and districts look like.

Having practitioners who are already doing this work help determine the ins and outs of the recognition systems is important, as those who are closest to it know what has worked, what has not, and what additional supports are needed. For example, in North Carolina, the Global Educator Digital Badge, Global Ready School, and Global Ready District designations were developed with external organizations that had a history of implementing global competence programs in schools (Tichnor-Wagner, 2016). Coupling capacity-building policies with funding is crucial. Otherwise, global competence becomes another "unfunded request" that schools and districts may brush aside because they don't think they can afford the professional development or teacher time out of the classroom.

Whether mandated or suggested, focused on capacity building or accountability, state and district leaders caution against having state policies that are too prescriptive. They have made these arguments for a number of reasons, not least of which is that global education is meant to be adaptive and responsive to students and the local context.

Higher Education Policies

Global competence can be integrated into teacher and leadership preparation programs that provide the pipeline of teachers and leaders to schools.

This can include coursework that infuses a global perspective, teaching abroad, and field experiences with diverse student populations and in schools that have a globally oriented mission and vision. It is important for global competence to be infused across programs of study within schools and colleges of education so it is not viewed as an "exclusive" program but is inclusive to all teachers and leaders (Gaudelli, 2016).

These policy needs are just a suggested place to start. As a school leader, you also have insights into what district, state, and university supports you might need to aid on-the-ground implementation in your specific context. Richard Elmore (1979) proposed that instead of starting from the perspective of the policymaker, policy design should start from the perspective of the person implementing that policy. To "backwards map" policy from practice, ask yourself, "What ability do I and my colleagues have to affect the global competence outcomes we want to see? What resources do we need to achieve the desired effect?" (p. 604). The answer to these questions becomes your policy ask: "We plan to do [insert global learning activity] so students can [insert student outcomes]. In order to do this, we will need [insert specific resources.]"

Once you have your policy needs articulated, ask away. Attend school board meetings. Talk to teacher preparation programs whose graduates you hire and whose student teachers you place in classrooms. Petition your state representatives. Tackle resistance you might receive with persistence. As the saying goes, if at first you don't succeed, try, try again. The worst-case scenario is that you spread awareness of an important cause, even if it stirs up some controversy. The best-case scenario? You help put in motion policy changes that will support schools across your district and state in providing a rigorous and relevant education for all students.

School leaders are the link that can bridge disparate "islands of excellence" —classrooms in which teachers are infusing deep, meaningful learning activities about the world—and taking these practices to scale. Our students have only lived in a world where diversity, digital connectivity, and global supply and demand are the norm. Our schools, whether we realize it or not, are caught up in the web of global interconnectedness. Regardless of whether you think globalization is a sign of progress or a force of negative disruption, globalization exists in the here and the now. The links between and among people, cultures, and economies are engrained in the companies, government institutions, and technologies we use every day.

The question should not be *whether* schools should teach students to navigate the complexities of globalization but *how* they should. Developing global competence in students, staff, and yourself cannot wait. It is time to lead the charge and ensure that each child receives a rigorous and relevant education grounded in our world.

References

Alfaro, C., & Quezada, R. L. (2010). International teacher professional development: Teacher reflections of authentic teaching and learning experiences. *Teaching Education, 21*(1), 47–59.

American Academy of Arts & Sciences. (2017). *America's languages: Investing in language education for the 21st century*. Cambridge, MA: Author.

American Federation of Teachers and Badass Teachers Association. (2017). *2017 Education Quality of Work Life Survey*. Washington, DC: Author. Retrieved from www.aft.org/sites/default/files/2017_eqwl_survey_web.pdf

Andreotti, V., & Pashby, K. (2013). Digital democracy and global citizenship education: Mutually compatible or mutually complicit? *The Educational Forum, 77*(4), 422–437.

Anti-Defamation League. (2007). Personal self-assessment of anti-bias behavior. Retrieved from www.adl.org/sites/default/files/documents/assets/pdf/education-outreach/Personal-Self-Assessment-of-Anti-Bias-Behavior.pdf

Anti-Defamation League. (2017a). Can we talk? Tips for respectful conversations in schools, workplaces, and communities. Retrieved from www.adl.org/education/resources/tools-and-strategies/can-we-talk-tips-for-respectful-conversations-in-schools#.WG0afH1nCRI

Anti-Defamation League. (2017b). Myths and facts about Muslim people and Islam. Retrieved from www.adl.org/education/resources/tools-and-strategies/myths-and-facts-about-muslim-people-and-islam

ASCD. (2016). *Global engagement survey*. Alexandria, VA: ASCD.

ASCD. (2017). The globally competent learning continuum. Retrieved from https://globallearning.ascd.org

ASCD. (2019). *The learning compact renewed: Whole child for the whole world*. Alexandria, VA: ASCD.

Asia Society. (n.d.). The global school design. Retrieved from https://asiasociety.org/education/global-school-design

Asia Society. (2009). *Going global: Preparing our students for an interconnected world*. Retrieved from http://asiasociety.org/files/Going%20Global%20Educator%20Guide.pdf

Aspen Institute National Commission on Social, Emotional, and Academic Development. (2019). From a nation at risk to a nation at hope: Recommendations from the National Commission on Social, Emotional, and Academic Development. Retrieved from http:// nationathope.org

Attendance Works & Johns Hopkins University. (2016). Preventing missed opportunity: Taking collective action to confront chronic absence. Retrieved from www .attendanceworks.org/preventing-missed-opportunity

Ball, S. J. (1998). Big policies/small world: An introduction to international perspectives in education policy. *Comparative Education, 34*(2), 119–130.

Banks, J. (2008). Diversity, group identity, and citizenship education in a global age. *Educational Researcher, 37*(3), 129–139.

Banks, J. (2017). *Citizenship education and global migration.* Washington, DC: American Educational Research Association.

Barbian, E., Gonzalez, G. C., & Mejia, P. (Eds). 2017. *Rethinking bilingual education: Welcoming home languages in our classrooms.* Milwaukee, WI: Rethinking Schools.

Baughman, L. M., & Francois, J. F. (2018). Trade and American jobs: The impact of trade on U.S. and state-level employment: 2018 update. Retrieved from http://tradepartnership. com/wp-content/uploads/2018/04/Trade-and-American-2018-FINAL-copy.pdf

Bishop, R. S. (1990). Mirrors, windows, and sliding doors. *Perspectives: Choosing and Using Books for the Classroom, 6*(3), ix–xi.

Borko, H. (2004). Professional development and teacher learning: Mapping the terrain. *Educational Researcher, 33*(8), 3–15.

Borko, H., Mayfield, V., Marion, S., Flexer, R., & Cumbo, K. (1997). Teachers' developing ideas and practices about mathematics performance assessment: Successes, stumbling blocks, and implications for professional development. *Teaching and Teacher Education, 13*(3), 259–278.

Brooks, J. S., & Normore, A. H. (2010). Educational leadership and globalization: Literacy for a global perspective. *Educational Policy, 24*(1), 52–82.

Bryk, A. S., Gomez, L. M., Grunow, A., & LeMahieu, P. G. (2015). *Learning to improve: How America's schools can get better at getting better.* Cambridge, MA: Harvard Education Press.

CASEL. (2019). Core SEL competencies. Retrieved from https://casel.org/core-competencies

Center for Teaching Quality & Digital Promise. (2016.) Micro-credentials: Driving teacher learning and leadership. Retrieved from https://digitalpromise.org/wp-content/ uploads/2016/06/Microcredentials_Driving_teacher_learning_leadership.pdf

Cheung, A. C. K., & Wong, P. M. (2011). Effects of school heads' and teachers' agreement with the curriculum reform on curriculum development progress and student learning in Hong Kong. *International Journal of Educational Management, 25*(5), 453–473.

Child Trends. (2018). Immigrant children. Retrieved from www.childtrends. org/?indicators=immigrant-children

Child Trends. (2019). Adverse experiences. Retrieved from www.childtrends. org/?indicators=adverse-experiences

Coburn, C. E. (2003). Rethinking scale: Moving beyond numbers to deep and lasting change. *Educational Researcher, 32*(6), 3–12.

Coburn, C. E., & Russell, J. L. (2008). District policy and teachers' social networks. *Educational Evaluation and Policy Analysis, 30*(3), 203–235.

Cohen, D. K., & Hill, H. C. (2001). *Learning policy: When state education reform works.* New Haven, CT: Yale University Press.

Collier, V. P., & Thomas, W. P. (2004). The astounding effectiveness of dual language education for all. *NABE Journal of Research and Practice, 2*(1), 1–20.

Committee for Economic Development. (2006). Education for global leadership: The importance of international studies and foreign language education for U.S. economic and national security. Washington, DC: Author. Retrieved from www.ced.org/pdf/Education-for-Global-Leadership.pdf

Cooper, B. S., & Fusarelli, B. C. (2009). Setting the stage: Where state power and education meet. In B.C. Fusarelli and B.S. Cooper (Eds.), *The rising state: How state power is transforming our nation's schools* (pp. 1–5). Albany, NY: SUNY Press.

Cruz, B. C., & Bermudez, P. R. (2009). Teacher education in the United States: A retrospective on the global awareness program at Florida International University. In T. F. Kirkwood-Tucker (Ed.), *Visions in global education* (pp. 90–115). New York: Peter Lang.

Cushner, K., & Brennan, S. (Eds.). (2007). *Intercultural student teaching: A bridge to global competence.* Lanham, MD: Rowman & Littlefield.

Darling-Hammond, L. (2010). *The flat world and education.* New York: Teachers College Press.

Datnow, A., Hubbard, L., & Mehan, H. (2002). *Extending educational reform: From one school to many.* New York: RoutledgeFalmer.

Davin, K. J., & Heineke, A. J. (2017). The seal of biliteracy: Variations in policy and outcomes. *Foreign Language Annals, 50*(3), 486–499.

Desimone, L. (2002). How can comprehensive school reform models be successfully implemented? *Review of Educational Research, 72*(3), 433–479.

DeVillar, R. A., & Jiang, B. (2012). From student teaching abroad to teaching in the U.S. classroom: Effects of global experiences on local instructional practice. *Teacher Education Quarterly, 39*(3), 7–24.

Devlin-Foltz, B. (2010). Teachers for the global age: A call to action for funders. *Teaching Education, 21*(1), 113–117.

Dolby, N., & Rahman, A. (2008). Research in international education. *Review of Educational Research, 78*(3), 676–726.

Duke, N. K., & Halvorsen, A. (2017, June 20.) New study shows the impact of PBL on student achievement. Retrieved from www.edutopia.org/article/new-study-shows-impact-pbl-student-achievement-nell-duke-anne-lise-halvorsen

Dunbar-Ortiz, R. (2014). *An indigenous peoples' history of the United States.* Boston: Beacon Press.

Elmore, R. F. (1979). Backward mapping: Implementation and policy design. *Political Science Quarterly, 94*(4), 601–616.

Elmore, R. F. (1996). Getting to scale with good educational practice. *Harvard Educational Review, 66*(1), 1–26.

Engel, L. (2018). K–12 study abroad linked with improved learning outcomes. *Education Week.* Retrieved from http://blogs.edweek.org/edweek/global_learning/2018/03/k-12_study_abroad_linked_with_improved_learning_outcomes.html?cmp=soc-edit-tw&print=1

Feinauer, E., & Howard, E. R. (2014). Attending to the third goal: Cross-cultural competence and identity development in two-way immersion programs. *Journal of Immersion and Content-Based Language Education, 2*(2), 257–272.

Frey, C. J., & Whitehead, D. (2009). International education policies and the boundaries of global citizenship in the US. *Journal of Curriculum Studies, 41*(2), 269–290.

Gallup, Inc. (2015). *2015 Gallup Student Poll.* Retrieved from www.gallupstudentpoll.com/188036/2015-gallup-student-poll-overall-report.aspx

Garcia, O, (2009). *Bilingual education in the 21st century: A global perspective.* West Sussex, UK: John Wiley & Sons.

Garet, M. S., Porter, A. C., Desimone, L., Birman, B. F., & Yoon, K. S. (2001). What makes professional development effective? Results from a national sample of teachers. *American Educational Research Journal, 38*(4), 915–945.

Gaudelli, W. (2003). *World class: Teaching and learning in global times.* Mahwah, NJ: Lawrence Erlbaum.

Gaudelli, W. (2009). Heuristics of global citizenship discourses towards curriculum enhancement. *Journal of Curriculum Theorizing, 25*(1), 68–85.

Gaudelli, W. (2016). *Global citizenship education: Everyday transcendence.* New York: Routledge.

Gay, G. (2010). *Culturally responsive teaching: Theory, research, and practice.* New York: Teachers College Press.

Gibbs, N. (2018). Why "listen" is the word of the year. Retrieved from https://medium.com/wordsthatmatter/why-listen-is-the-word-of-the-year-7136ffee99c5

Gibson, M. A. (1998). Promoting academic success among immigrant students: Is acculturation the issue? *Educational Policy, 12*(6), 615–633.

Goldenberg, C., & Wagner, K. (2015). Bilingual education. *American Educator.* Retrieved from www.aft.org/ae/fall2015/goldenberg_wagner

Greenfield, P. M. (1997). You can't take it with you: Why ability assessments don't cross cultures. *American Psychologist, 52*(10), 1115–1124.

Guskey, T. R. (2002). Professional development and teacher change. *Teachers and Teaching, 8*(3), 381–391.

Guskey, T. R. (2003). Analyzing lists of the characteristics of effective professional development to promote visionary leadership. *NASSP Bulletin, 87*(637), 4–20.

Hasso Plattner Institute of Design at Stanford. (n.d.). Guide for creating a design challenge. Retrieved from https://dschool-old.stanford.edu

Hatch, T. (2001). Incoherence in the system: Three perspectives on the implementation of multiple initiatives in one district. *American Journal of Education, 109*(4), 407–437.

High Quality Project Based Learning. (n.d.) A framework for high quality project-based learning. Retrieved from https://hqpbl.org

Holm, M. (2011). Project-based instruction: A review of the literature on effectiveness in prekindergarten. *River Academic Journal, 7*(2), 1–13.

Honig, M. I., & Hatch, T. C. (2004). Crafting coherence: How schools strategically manage multiple, external demands. *Educational Researcher, 33,* 16–30.

Ingber, S. (2017). Science loving teens from Ghana and D.C. geek out together. *NPR.* Retrieved from www.npr.org/sections/goatsandsoda/2017/03/23/520864034/science-loving-teens-from-ghana-and-d-c-geek-out-together

Institute of International Education. (2018). Fields of study of U.S. study abroad students, 2006/07–2016/17. Open doors report on international educational exchange. Retrieved from www.iie.org/opendoors

Intergovernmental Panel on Climate Change. (2018). Global warming of 1.5 degree C. Paris: United Nations. Retrieved from www.ipcc.ch/sr15.

International Organization for Migration. (2017). *World migration report 2018.* Retrieved from www.iom.int/wmr/world-migration-report-2018

Jackson, A. (2011). Redesigning schools for work and citizenship in a global era. In *Educating America's Youth for Success in the Global Arena* (pp. 63–70): Washington, DC: Aspen Institute.

Jean-Marie, G., Normore, A. H., & Brooks, J. S. (2009). Leadership for social justice: Preparing 21st century school leaders for a new social order. *Journal of Research on Leadership Education, 4*(1), 1–31.

Johnson, L. (2007). Rethinking successful school leadership in challenging U.S. schools: Culturally responsive practices in school-community relationships. *International Studies in Educational Administration, 35*(3), 49–57.

Jordan, P. W., & Marley, P. (2018). How did ESSA's "non-academic" indicator get so academic? Washington, DC: FutureEd. Retrieved from www.future-ed.org/how-did-essas-non-academic-indicator-get-so-academic

Kirkwood, T. F. (2001). Our global age requires global education: Clarifying definitional ambiguities. *The Social Studies, 92*(1), 10–15.

Klem, A. M., & Connell, J. P. (2004). Relationships matter: Linking teacher support to student engagement and achievement. *Journal of School Health, 74*(7), 262–273.

Kokotsaki, D., Menzies, V., & Wiggins, A. (2016) Project-based learning: A review of the literature. *Improving Schools, 19*(3), 267–277.

Kuenzi, J. J. (2018). Teacher preparation policies and issues in the Higher Education Act. Washington, DC: Congressional Research Service. Retrieved from https://fas.org/sgp/crs/misc/R45407.pdf

Labaree, D. E. (1997). Public goods, private goods: The American struggle over educational goals. *American Education Research Journal, 34*(1), 39–81.

Ladson-Billings, G. (1995). Toward a theory of culturally relevant pedagogy. *American Educational Research Journal, 32,* 465–491.

Leachman, M., & Figueroa, E. (2019). K–12 school funding up in most 2019 teacher-protest states, but still well below decade ago. Washington, DC: Center on Budget and Policy Priorities. Retrieved from www.cbpp.org/research/state-budget-and-tax/k-12-school-funding-up-in-most-2018-teacher-protest-states-but-still

Leachman, M., Masterson, K., & Figueroa, E. (2017). A punishing decade for school funding. *Center on Budget and Policy Priorities*. Retrieved from www.cbpp.org/research/state-budget-and-tax/a-punishing-decade-for-school-funding

Leithwood, K., & Jantzi, D. (2006). Transformational school leadership for large-scale reform: Effects on students, teachers, and their classroom practices. *School Effectiveness and School Improvement, 17*(2), 201–227.

Leithwood, K., Louis, K. S., Anderson, S., & Wahlstrom, K. (2004). Review of research: How leadership influences student learning. Retrieved from https:// conservancy.umn.edu/bitstream/handle/11299/2035/CAREI?sequence=1

Lindsay, J. (2016). *The global educator.* Eugene: OR: International Society for Technology in Education.

Little, J. W. (2002). Professional community and the problem of high school reform. *International Journal of Educational Research, 37*, 693–714.

Louis, K. S., Marks, H. M., & Kruse, S. (1996). Teachers' professional community in restructuring schools. *American Educational Research Journal, 33*(4), 757–798.

Mahon, J. (2010) Fact or fiction? Analyzing institutional barriers and individual responsibility to advance the internationalization of teacher education. *Teaching Education, 21*(1), 7–18.

Mahon, J., & Cushner, K. (2007). The impact of overseas student teaching on personal and professional development. In K. Cushner and S. Brennan (Eds.), *Intercultural student teaching: A bridge to global competence* (pp. 57–87). Lanham, MD: Rowman & Littlefield.

Mahtani, S., & Wutwanich, P. (2018, July 10). A miracle, a science, or what: How the world came together to save 12 boys trapped in a Thai cave. *The Washington Post.* Retrieved from https://wapo.st/2uj6eQQ?tid=ss_tw

Mann, B. (2014, March 12). Equity and equality are not equal. Washington, DC: The Education Trust. Retrieved from https://edtrust.org/the-equity-line/equity-and-equality-are-not-equal

Mansilla, V. B. (2016). How to be a global thinker. *Educational Leadership, 74*(4), 10–16.

Mansilla, V. B., & Jackson. A. (2011). *Educating for global competence: Preparing our youth to engage the world.* Retrieved from https://asiasociety.org/files/book-globalcompetence.pdf

Manza, J., & Crowley, N. (2018). Ethnonationalism and the Rise of Donald Trump. *Contexts, 17*(1), 28–33.

Marks, H. M., & Printy, S. M. (2003). Principal leadership and school performance: An integration of transformational and instructional leadership. *Educational Administration Quarterly, 39*(3), 370–397.

Marshall, C., & Gerstl-Pepin, C. (2005). *Re-framing educational politics for social justice.* Boston: Pearson Education.

Massachusetts Department of Elementary and Secondary Education. (2018). *Massachusetts model system for educator evaluation: Classroom teacher rubric.* Retrieved from www.doe.mass.edu/edeval/model/PartIII_AppxC.pdf

McLaughlin, M. (1990). The RAND change agent study revisited: Macro perspectives and micro realities. *Educational Researcher, 19,* 11–16.

McLaughlin, M. W., & Talbert, J. E. (2001). *Professional communities and the world of high school teaching.* Chicago: University of Chicago Press.

Moll, L. C., Amanti, C., Neff, D., & Gonzalez, N. (1992). Funds of knowledge for teaching: Using a qualitative approach to connect homes and classrooms. *Theory into Practice, 31*(2), 132–141.

Muller, G. C. (2012). *Exploring characteristics of international schools that promote international-mindedness.* Doctoral dissertation, Teachers College, Columbia University.

National Association for Media Literacy Education. (2007). Key questions to ask when analyzing media messages. Retrieved from https://namle.net/publications/core-principles

National Center for Children in Poverty. (2018). Basic facts about low-income children: Children under 18, 2016. Retrieved from www.nccp.org/publications/pub_1194.html

National Center for Education Statistics. (2015–2016). *National teacher and principal survey.* Washington, DC: U.S. Department of Education. Retrieved from https://nces.ed.gov/surveys/ntps/tables/ntps1516_20180404001_t1n.asp

National Policy Board of Educational Administration. (2015). *Professional standards for educational leaders.* Reston, VA: Author. Retrieved from http://npbea.org/wp-content/uploads/2017/06/Professional-Standards-for-Educational-Leaders_2015.pdf

Newmann, F. M., Smith, B., Allensworth, E., & Bryk, A. S. (2001). Instructional program coherence: What it is and why it should guide school improvement policy. *Educational Evaluation and Policy Analysis, 23*(4), 297–321.

Noddings, N. (1984). *Caring: A relational approach to ethics and moral education.* Berkeley: University of California Press.

North Carolina Department of Public Instruction. (2015). *Global educator digital badge criteria for other educators.* Retrieved from www.ncpublicschools.org/docs/globaled/actions/add-criteria.pdf

OECD. (2018). The future of education and skills: Education 2030. The future we want. Paris: OECD. Retrieved from www.oecd.org/education/2030/learning-framework-2030.htm

OECD and Asia Society. (2018). *Teaching for global competence in a rapidly changing world.* Paris: OECD Publishing.

Paris, D. (2012). Culturally sustaining pedagogy: A needed change in stance, terminology, and practice. *Educational Researcher, 41*(3), 93–97.

Parkhouse, H., Tichnor-Wagner, A., Glazier, J., & Cain, J. M. (2016). "You don't have to travel the world": Accumulating experiences on the path toward globally competent teaching. *Teaching Education, 27*(3), 267–285.

Peacock, J. L. (2007). *Grounded globalism: How the U.S. south embraces the world.* Athens, GA: University of Georgia Press.

Perrier, C. (2017). Teaching U.N. sustainability goals to create global citizens. *Education Week*. Retrieved from https://blogs.edweek.org/edweek/global_learning/2017/04/teaching_the_un_sustainable_development_goals_through_project_based_learning.html

Poole, C. M., & Russell III, W. B. (2015). Educating for global perspectives: A study of teacher preparation programs. *Journal of Education, 195*(3), 41–52.

Potok, M. (2017). The year in hate and extremism. Southern Poverty Law Center. Retrieved from www.splcenter.org/fighting-hate/intelligence-report/2017/year-hate-and-extremism

Primary Source. (2017). Primary Source's elements of a global school. Retrieved from www.primarysource.org/file/PS_Elements_of_a_Global_School.pdf

Public Schools of North Carolina. (2013). *North Carolina professional teaching standards*. Retrieved from www.ncpublicschools.org/docs/effectiveness-model/ncees/standards/prof-teach-standards.pdf

Reimers, F. (2009a). Educating for global competency. In *International Perspectives on the Goals of Universal Basic Secondary Education*, by J. E. Cohen and M. B. Malin (Eds.). Cambridge, MA: American Academy of Arts and Sciences.

Reimers, F. (2009b). Leading for global competency. *Educational Leadership, 67*(1). Retrieved from www.ascd.org/publications/educational-leadership/sept09/vol67/num01/Leading-for-Global-Competency.aspx

Reimers, F. (2017). *Empowering students to improve the world in 60 lessons: Version 1.0*. CreateSpace Independent Publishing Platform.

Robertson, R. (1995). Glocalization: Time-space and homogeneity. In M. Featherstone, S. Lash, and R. Robertson (Eds.), *Global Modernity* (pp. 25–44). London: Sage.

Rodberg, S. (2016). The culture friendly school. *Educational Leadership, 74*(4), 66–69.

Rothstein-Fisch, C., & Trumbull, E. (2008). *Managing diverse classrooms: How to build on students' cultural strengths*. Alexandria, VA: ASCD.

Sahlberg, P. (2006). Education reform for raising economic competitiveness. *Journal of Educational Change, 7*(4), 259–287.

Singmaster, H. (2012, August 15). Make service learning global. *Education Week*. Retrieved from https://blogs.edweek.org/edweek/global_learning/2012/08/make_service_learning_global.html

Smolcic, E., & Katunich, J. (2017). Teachers crossing borders: A review of the research into cultural immersion field experience for teachers. *Teaching and Teacher Education, 62*, 47–59.

Sodexo. (2015). *2015 workplace trends*. Retrieved from https://uk.sodexo.com/home/media/news-room/newsList-area/uk-press-releases/sodexo-workplace-trends-report-2.html

Spillane, J. P. (2005). Distributed leadership. *The Educational Forum* 69(2), 143–150.

Spillane, J. P., Reiser, B. J., & Reimer, T. (2002). Policy implementation and cognition: Reframing and refocusing implementation research. *Review of Educational Research, 72*(3), 387–431.

Spring, J. (2010). *American education* (14th ed.). Boston: McGraw-Hill Higher Education.

Staudt, B. (2016). Developing global competency skills in grades 9–12: Implications for school leadership. [Unpublished doctoral dissertation]. Williamsburg, VA: College of William and Mary.

Steele, J. L., Slater, R. O., Zamarro, G., Miller, T., Li, J., Burkhauser, S., et al., (2017). Effects of dual-language immersion programs on student achievement: Evidence from lottery data. *American Educational Research Journal, 54*(1_suppl), 282S–306S.

Stewart. V. (2010). A classroom as wide as the world. In H. H. Jacobs (Ed.), *Curriculum 21: Essential Curriculum for a Changing World* (pp. 97–114). Alexandria, VA: ASCD.

Stringfield, S., & Datnow, A. (2002). Systemic supports for schools serving students placed at risk. In S. Stringfield & D. Land (Eds.), *Educating At-Risk Students* (pp. 269–288). Chicago: National Society for the Study of Education.

Stringfield, S., Datnow, A., Ross, S. M., & Snively, F. (1998). Scaling up school restructuring in multicultural, multilingual contexts: Early observations from Sunland County. *Education and Urban Society, 30*, 326–357.

Teaching Tolerance. (2011). Ten myths about immigration. *Teaching Tolerance, 39*. Retrieved from www.tolerance.org/magazine/spring-2011/ten-myths-about-immigration

Terrazas, A. (2011). Immigrants in new destination states. Washington, DC *Migration Policy Institute*. Retrieved from www.migrationpolicy.org/article/immigrants-new-destination-states.

Tichnor-Wagner, A. (2016). Global education politics and policy: Discourses, coalitions, and co-construction among globally committed national, state, and district actors. (Unpublished doctoral dissertation). University of North Carolina at Chapel Hill: Chapel Hill, NC.

Tichnor-Wagner, A. (2019). Globally minded leadership: A new approach for leading schools in diverse democracies. *International Journal of Education Policy and Leadership, 15*(2). Retrieved from http://journals.sfu.ca/ijepl/index.php/ijepl/article/view/869/194

Tichnor-Wagner, A., Allen, D., Socol, A. R., Cohen-Vogel, L., Rutledge, S., & Xing, Q. (2018). Studying implementation within a continuous improvement process: What happens when we design with adaptations in mind? *Teachers College Record, 120*(5), 1–52.

Tichnor-Wagner, A., Harrison, C., & Cohen-Vogel, L. (2016). Cultures of learning in effective high schools. *Educational Administration Quarterly, 52*(4), 602–642.

Tichnor-Wagner, A., & Manise, J. (2019). *Globally competent educational leadership: A framework for leading schools in a diverse, interconnected world.* Alexandria, VA: ASCD and Longview Foundation. Retrieved from http://files.ascd.org/pdfs/publications/general/ascd-globally-competent-educational-leadership-report-2019.pdf

Tichnor-Wagner, A., Parkhouse, H., Glazier, J., & Cain, J. M. (2016). Expanding approaches to teaching for diversity and justice: Fostering global citizenship across content areas. *Education Policy Analysis Archives, 24*(59), 1–35.

Tichnor-Wagner, A., Parkhouse, H., Glazier, J., & Cain, J. M. (2019). *Becoming a globally competent teacher.* Alexandria, VA: ASCD.

Tichnor-Wagner, A., & Socol, A.R. (2016). The presidential platform on twenty-first century education goals. *Education Policy Analysis Archives, 25*(64), 1-32.

Trust, T. (2012). Professional learning networks designed for teacher learning. *Journal of Digital Learning in Teacher Education, 28*(4), 133–138.

Tucker, M. (2016.) Global ready—or not? *Educational Leadership, 74*(4), 30–35.

Tyack, D., & Cuban, L. (1995). *Tinkering toward utopia: A century of public school reform.* Cambridge, MA: Harvard University Press.

UNESCO. (2015). Global citizenship education: Topics and learning objectives. Retrieved from http://unesdoc.unesco.org/images/0023/002329/232993e.pdf

United Nations. (2018). One in five children, adolescents, and youth is out of school. Fact Sheet No. 48. February 2018. Retrieved from http://uis.unesco.org/en/news/education-data-release-one-every-five-children-adolescents-and-youth-out-school

United Nations. (2019). Sustainable development goals. Retrieved from www.un.org/sustainabledevelopment

United Nations Climate Change. (2019). What is the Paris Agreement? Retrieved from https://unfccc.int/process-and-meetings/the-paris-agreement/what-is-the-paris-agreement

U.S. Department of Education. (2012). *Succeeding globally through international education and engagement: U.S. Department of Education international strategy 2012–16.* Retrieved from www2.ed.gov/about/inits/ed/internationaled/international-strategy-2012-16.pdf

U.S. Department of Education. (2016). *Non-regulatory guidance for Title II, Part A: Building systems of support for excellent teaching and leading.* Retrieved from www2.ed.gov/policy/elsec/leg/essa/essatitleiipartaguidance.pdf

U.S. Department of Education. (2017). Framework for developing global and cultural competencies to advance equity, excellence, and economic competitiveness. Retrieved from https://sites.ed.gov/international/global-and-cultural-competency

U.S. Department of State. (2019). Bureau of Educational and Cultural Affairs Exchange Programs. Retrieved from https://exchanges.state.gov/us/program/fulbright-distinguished-awards-teaching-us-teachers

Valenzuela, A. (1999). *Subtractive schooling: US-Mexican youth and the politics of caring.* Albany, NY: State University of New York Press.

Vara-Orta, F. (2017). Hate in schools. *Education Week.* Retrieved from www.edweek.org/ew/projects/hate-in-schools.html

Vygotsky, L. (1978). Interaction between learning and development. *Readings on the development of children, 23*(3), 34–41.

Wahlstrom, K. L., & Louis, K. S. (2008). How teachers experience principal leadership: The roles of professional community, trust, efficacy, and shared responsibility. *Educational Administration Quarterly, 44*(4), 458–495.

Walton, G. M., & Spencer, S. J. (2009). Latent ability: Grades and test scores systematically underestimate the intellectual ability of negatively stereotyped students. *Psychological Science, 20*(9), 1132–1139.

Weick, K. E. (1976). Educational organizations as loosely coupled systems. *Administrative Science Quarterly, 21,* 1–18.

Wiley, B. (2013). Promoting global competence: Factors that influence the development of an international studies high school. (Unpublished doctoral dissertation). The University of Pennsylvania, Philadelphia, PA.

Wiley, D. (2001). Forty years of the Title VI and Fulbright-Hayes international education programs. In P. O'Meara, H. D. Mehlinger, and R. M. Newman (Eds.), *Changing perspectives in international education* (pp. 11–29). Bloomington, IN: Indiana University Press.

World Economic Forum. (2018). *Future of jobs report 2018.* Geneva, Switzerland: Author. Retrieved from www.weforum.org/reports/the-future-of-jobs-report-2018

Zeichner, N. (2015). Why teacher leaders are critical to advancing global education. *Education Week.* Retrieved from http://blogs.edweek.org/edweek/global_learning/2015/08/why_teacher_leaders_are_critical_to_advancing_global_education.html

Zeigler, K., & Camarota, S. A. (2018). Almost half speak a foreign language in America's largest cities. *Center for Immigration Studies.* Retrieved from https://cis.org/Report/Almost-Half-Speak-Foreign-Language-Americas-Largest-Cities#3

Zong, G. (2009). Global perspectives in teacher education research and practice. In T. F. Kirkwood-Tucker (Ed.), *Visions in global education* (pp. 215–239). New York: Peter Lang.

Index

The letter *f* following a page number denotes a figure.

About the Author

**Ariel Tichnor-Wagner** is a lecturer in the Educational Leadership and Policy Studies program at Boston University and coauthor of the book *Becoming a Globally Competent Teacher*. Formerly the Senior Fellow of Global Competence at ASCD, she advocates for, develops, and implements innovative frameworks, tools, and professional learning experiences that support educators in fostering the knowledge, skills, and attitudes students need to succeed in a diverse, interconnected world. Ariel began her career as an elementary school teacher in a high-poverty school district in Phoenix, Arizona, where she taught primarily English language learners. She has also led student trips and volunteered in educational programs in Nicaragua, Guatemala, Costa Rica, Peru, and Israel. She graduated summa cum laude with a BA in history from the University of Pennsylvania. She received a master's degree in Elementary Education from Arizona State University and a doctoral degree in Education Policy, Leadership, and School Improvement from the University of North Carolina at Chapel Hill. As an educator and researcher, she is committed to identifying and leveraging policies and practices that improve academic and social-emotional outcomes of culturally and linguistically diverse students and that foster global citizenship. Her writing on global competence and school improvement has appeared in a variety of outlets, including *Education Week, Educational Administration Quarterly, Leadership and Policy in Schools, Journal of Educational Change, Teaching Education, Education Policy Analysis Archives,* and *Educational Policy.*

Related ASCD Resources: Global Competence

At the time of publication, the following resources were available (ASCD stock numbers in parentheses). For up-to-date information about ASCD resources, go to www.ascd.org. You can search the complete archives of *Educational Leadership* at www.ascd.org/el.

Print Products

All Teaching Is Social and Emotional: Helping Students Develop Essential Skills for the Classroom and Beyond by Nancy Frey, Douglas Fisher, and Dominique Smith (#119033)

Becoming a Globally Competent Teacher by Ariel Tichnor-Wagner, Hillary Parkhouse, Jocelyn Glazier, and J. Montana Cain (#119012)

Building Equity: Policies and Practices to Empower All Learners by Dominique Smith, Nancy E. Frey, Ian Pumpian, and Douglas E. Fisher (#117031)

Catching Up or Leading the Way: American Education in the Age of Globalization by Yong Zhao (#109076)

How to Teach Now: Five Keys to Personalized Learning in the Global Classroom by William Powelll and Ochan Kusuma-Powell (#111011)

Keeping It Real and Relevant: Building Authentic Relationships in Your Diverse Classroom by Ignacio Lopez (#117049)

Using Understanding by Design in the Culturally and Linguistically Diverse Classroom by Amy J. Heineke and Jay McTighe (#118084)

ASCD myTeachSource®

Download resources from a professional learning platform with hundreds of research-based best practices and tools for your classroom at http://myteachsource.ascd.org/.

For more information, send an e-mail to member@ascd.org; call 1-800-933-2723 or 703-578-9600; send a fax to 703-575-5400; or write to Information Services, ASCD, 1703 N. Beauregard St., Alexandria, VA 22311-1714 USA.

WHOLE CHILD
TENETS

The ASCD Whole Child approach is an effort to transition from a focus on narrowly defined academic achievement to one that promotes the long-term development and success of all children. Through this approach, ASCD supports educators, families, community members, and policymakers as they move from a vision about educating the whole child to sustainable, collaborative actions.

Becoming a Globally Competent School Leader relates to the **engaged**, **supported**, and **challenged** tenets.

For more about the ASCD Whole Child approach, visit **www.ascd.org/wholechild.**

1 HEALTHY
Each student enters school healthy and learns about and practices a healthy lifestyle.

2 SAFE
Each student learns in an environment that is physically and emotionally safe for students and adults.

3 ENGAGED
Each student is actively engaged in learning and is connected to the school and broader community.

4 SUPPORTED
Each student has access to personalized learning and is supported by qualified, caring adults.

5 CHALLENGED
Each student is challenged academically and prepared for success in college or further study and for employment and participation in a global environment.

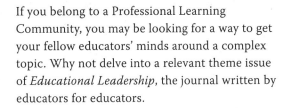